Anantha Murthy's

SAMSKARA

CELEBRATING INDIAN LITERATURE

Anantha Murthy's

SAMSKARA

edited and introduced by

RASHMI GAUR

Prestige

an international publishing house

Published by
Prestige Books
3/28, East Patel Nagar
New Delhi 110 008
Ph. 9818755529

ISBN: 81-7851-023-5

Printed at Chaman Offset Press, New Delhi 110 002

Contents

U.R. Anantha Murthy's *Samskara*: A Textual Analysis and Comprehensive Discussion by Rashmi Gaur

Critical Perspectives

U.R. Anantha Murthy: Life and Works

RASHMI GAUR
Indian Institute of Technology, Roorkee

Udupi Rajagopala Acharya Anantha Murthy is one of the most important representatives of the new movement in the literature of the Kannada language and is counted among the most eminent Indian authors. He has been the winner of a number of awards both from the Government and also Academies for his invaluable contribution in different fields. In 1998 he was awarded with the prestigious Padma Bhushan award. In 1994 he won the Jnanapeeth, India's highest literary award. Besides these, he has won other awards including the Literary Distinction, awarded by the Government of Karnataka in 1984. Karnataka Sahitya Akaemi conferred the Fiction Award and Award for Literary Achievement, in the year 1983 and 1984 respectively. He won the Masti Award in Literature in the year 1994. He is also the winner of the Ganakrishti Award for Literary Distinction, Kolkatta, for the year 2002. Besides these, he has been the winner of a number of awards from the Karnataka Film Development Corporation for best stories like *Samskara*, *Ghatashradda*, *Bara* etc. at different times.

U.R. Anantha Murthy was born on December 21, 1932 at Melige, a remote Village in Tirthahalli Taluka, in Shimoga District. He is the product of a rare mixed education because he was born into a traditional Brahmin family and was educated in Sanskrit and Kannada as well as in English. He had his early education in Durvasamatha Sanskrit school. He had his later education in Thirthahalli and Mysore. He completed his graduation and post-graduation from the University of Mysore. After doing his post-graduation in English literature, he went to England for higher studies. In 1966, he earned Ph.D. in English and Comparative Literature from the University of Birmingham, U.K. for his thesis on "English and Comparative literature." Here he worked with Malcolm Bradbury, David Lodge, and Raymond Williams.

He began his career as a Lecturer in English in 1956 at Mysore University and later became a Professor. A distinguished scholar, he has taught at various universities in Europe and the United States. He has served as a Visiting Professor at the Cornell University (2001), University of Iowa (1975), Shivaji University, Kolhapur (1982), University of Tubingen, Germany (1992), University of Pennsylvania (2000), University of Hyderabad (2001), and many other universities. During the period 1987 to 1990, he served as the Vice-Chancellor of Mahatma Gandhi University, Kottayam. Besides, he has also served as the Chairman of the National Book Trust of India at Delhi in 1992-93, Indian Institute of Social Sciences in 1998 and The Film and Television Institute of India at Pune in 2002. He was the President of the Sahitya Akademi from 1993 to 1998.

U.R. Anantha Murthy is also well-known for his oratory. He has travelled widely around the globe. He has undertaken innumerable tours, attended several national and international conferences and has given a number of lectures on various topics since 1974. He undertook tours as an Indian delegate to West Germany in 1988 representing University Grants Commission. As a cultural representative he visited North Korea and Republic of China in 1998. He visited Moscow as member of the International Advisory Board of *Inostrannaya Litteratura* (Soviet Monthly) in 1989. In the year 2002 he visited Book Festivals at France, Berlin and Munich.

He has delivered lectures on varied areas such as politics, culture, literature, art and a number of other issues. Important ones to be noted are the lecture on "Culture and Destiny," given at Bharat Bhavan, Bhopal, "Indian Literature," at the University of Madison and Chicago in 1985, "Indian Society, Culture, Politics, and Literature" delivered at the University of Birmingham, Alabama in 1987, "Colonialism and Indian Literature" delivered at University of California, "Art in the Modern Age" at Bangalore University in 1989. He has served on many important committees as Member and Chairman. He has interviewed many celebrities for television and documentaries.

The creative genius of U.R. Anantha Murthy is reflected in his prolific writings. Majority of his writing is in Kannada. His works can be classified into stories, poems, novels and essays. He began his literary career in 1955 with the story volume *Endendhigu Mugiyada Kathe*. Other story collections include works like *Mauni* (1967), *Prashne* (1962), *Akasha Mattu Bekku* (1983), *Mooru Dasakada Kathegalu* (1989), *Suryana Kudure* (1995) and *Aidu Dashakada Kathegalu* (2001). His poetry collections like *Mithuna* (1992), *Ajjana Hegala Sukkugalu* (1989), *15 Padyagalu* (1967), *Eeevareginal Kavithegalu* (2001), *Eeevareginal Kavithegalu* (2001) have gripped the imagination of the readers. His essays include *Prajne Mattu Parisara* (literary and philosophical essays), *Samakshama* (essays on politics, culture, society, literature), *Yuga Pallata* (Essays), *Abhinava* (2001) *Kannada, Karnataka* (selected essays 2001). His novels include *Samskara* (1965), which has been translated into English, Russian, French, Hungarian, German, Swedish, Hindi, Bengali, Malayalam, Marathi, Urdu, Tamil and Gujarati; *Bharathipura* (1974), *Divya* (2001) and others.

His contribution to English language is no way less than to Kannada. Many of his works in Kannada have been translated into English by different authors. For instance, 'Initiation' is a Kannada story translated by Gary Wills, *Avasthe* a novel, translated by Shanthinath Desai, *Bhava and Twenty Vachanas from Sunya Sampadane* is a set of twenty poems translated from Kannada by Judith Kroll; *Bharathipura*, a novel, has been translated by P. Srinivasa Rao. The other works in English include essays on various topics like "Literature and Culture" (2002), "The Concept of Man in Kannada Literature" (1979) and others. At present U.R. Anantha Murthy is settled in Bangalore.

Anantha Murthy's short novel *Samskara* created a big furore in Karnataka when it was published more than thirty years ago. With this novel Anantha Murthy, a brahmin himself, held aloft a mirror to the brahmin community. It has been translated into Hindi, Bengali, Telugu, Tamil, Urdu, Marathi, Oriya, Gujarati and Konkani languages of India. It has also been translated into several European languages including English, French, Russian, Hungarian, German and Kazak. In 1970 it was made into a movie of the same name by Girish Karnad and was crowned with many awards including the President's Gold medal. It is one of the few art films of its kind in the Kannada language and started a new wave of author films in India.

The novel raises the question of defining the essence of culture—is it achieved by blindly following rules and traditions, is it lost when they are not kept? The background for this eternal question, which actually remains unresolved even in this novel, is the *Samskara* (funeral) of Naranappa, a brahmin who rejected his brahminhood. (Among the several meanings of the word *Samskara*, some of the important ones are culture, funeral and ritual). Anantha Murthy based the story on a village that was very much like the village of his childhood where tensions between tradition and modernity emerged daily in people's experiences. Against its background, he questions discrimination through the caste system and the repressive beliefs/practices of the Brahmins. The novel revolutionised the orthodox concepts of a community in Karnataka. As a religious novel about a decaying brahmin colony in the south Indian village of Karnataka, it serves as an allegory rich in realistic detail, a contemporary reworking of ancient Hindu themes and myths, and a serious, poetic study of a religious man living in a community of priests gone to seed. A death which stands as the central event in the plot brings in its wake a plague, many more deaths, live questions with only dead answers, moral chaos, and the rebirth of one man.

Bharatiputra (1973) is another famous novel by U.R. Anantha Murthy which, like *Samskara*, has also become a classic. In this novel Jagannatha, the Brahmin and landowner, goes back to his hometown, after studies in England. His hometown is highly traditional in its values and he tries to change its social structures. He wants to enable the untouchables to enter the temple and with this meets the resistance of the higher castes. His attempt to create a just system around him and with this, inner freedom, fails. Anantha Murthy deliberately writes in Kannada and not in English.

Anantha Murthy is known far beyond the Indian language borders and abroad on account of his books and social engagements. The themes which are his central focus are the examination of the caste system, religious rules and traditions as well as the ambivalent relationship between the handed down cultural value system and the new values of a changing world. In both his fiction and essays, he tries to demolish the hegemonic power structures that canons impose on us.

Samskara: A Thematic Analysis of the Novel

RASHMI GAUR

The title of the novel, *Samskara*, significantly conveys the presence of a multifaceted reality against an allegorical backdrop. This multi-vocal Sanskrit word conveys as many as nine different meanings, explained in the epigraph, which implicitly inform the action. Furthermore, "the action depends on the several meanings being at loggerheads with each other."[1] The realistic details of the plot are often dominated by the richness of allegorical interpretations, as the novel dramatizes moral dilemmas concerning the body.

Part I

Chapter I

The first chapter of the novel begins with a description of the seemingly inflexible daily routine of Praneshacharya, a *Madhva* brahmin, who is the spiritual head of the brahmins of Durbasapura, and also the protagonist of the novel. First few paragraphs show how carefully he looks after his invalid wife Bhagirathi. Several traits of his characters are visible immediately. Readers are told of "a twenty year old routine" (1) between Praneshacharya and his wife Bhagirathi. Being an invalid, she is entirely dependent on her husband. Her body has shrivelled owing to her illness and has been compared with a "dried-up wasted pea-pod." (1) Praneshacharya lives the life of a celibate householder. At the age of sixteen, he had opted for marriage in accordance with the scriptural injunction, but had deliberately chosen a bed-ridden, invalid and sick woman for wife. He serves her placidly. However, it is evident that his administrations to his wife are a result of a well-rehearsed habit and lack spontaneity. His compassion for his wife—bathing and feeding her, humorous indulgence with her repeated entreaties for possessing a second wife—is not the selfless love of a devoted husband; it is a penance which shall facilitate his ultimate *nirvana*. He implicitly follows the teaching of the *Bhagvadgita*, "Do what is to be done with no thought of fruit." In order to attain salvation, he is ready to undergo all kinds of tests. He is proud of his sacrifice.

Praneshacharya also possesses an exemplary reputation as a learned priest and preceptor in his community and also among neighbouring Brahmin communities. The Brahmins of the agrahara come daily to his house to listen to his recitation of sacred legends, "always new and always dear to them and to him." (1) Addressing the Brahmins is also established as an inflexible schedule "before a ripple is allowed to form in his stagnant life by the announcement of a death."[2]

After a rudimentary introduction of Praneshacharya, readers are told of Naranappa's death. Naranappa is an intriguing character who has been termed as the other *famous* Brahmin of the agrahara. He had rejected his brahminhood and was openly living with Chandri, a lowcaste prostitute, whom he had brought from Kundapura, a nearby town. Chandri agitatedly announces Naranappa's death to Praneshacharya. Though she is unaware of the fact that he had died of bubonic plague, she describes the symptoms accurately, "Four days of fever, that's all. He had a painful lump on his side, the kind they get with fever." (3)

The manner in which Anantha Murthy has depicted this episode underscores the severity of caste discrimination practised in the traditional Indian society. Chandri's presence is not welcome in a Brahmin household. She is an untouchable, her very presence is polluting for the upper caste people who are obsessed with physical and mental purity. "If the Acharya talked to her, he would be polluted, he would have to bathe again before his meal." (2) Still, the Acharya immediately responds and on hearing of Naranappa's death, goes to call Garudacharya and other kinsmen. It is still early in the day, the brahmins haven't taken their meals. Now they will not be able to take food till the last rites—the *Samskaras*—of the dead man are performed.

Naranappa's death creates an anxiety among the brahmin families of the agrahara. Alive, he was "an enemy; dead, a preventer of meals; as a corpse, a problem, a nuisance." (3) Praneshacharya brings the problem to the fore—Naranappa's death rites have to be performed, but who should do it, as he had no children of his own? In the absence of any relative, any brahmin can offer to perform the last rites. In the absence of a direct heir, the Brahmin performing the last rites shall also inherit the dead man's property. This possibility initiates crude, selfish calculations by various brahmins and their wives. Garudacharya and Lakshmanna, who were kins of Naranappa, question his brahminhood. Naranappa not only lived with a lowcaste concubine, he also ate the food cooked by her, drank spirits, and also enjoyed animal flesh with his Muslim friends. Traditional caste taboos laid a significant emphasis on the sharing of food. The higher caste people considered the food prepared by the untouchables as impure and were encouraged to reject it. Naranappa had violated these injunctions. He also did not observe the death anniversaries of his parents. Such behaviour indicates his rejection of the Brahmin faith. Praneshacharya however declares that though Naranappa was practically ostracized, he "did not die an outcaste" and hence only another brahmin has a right to touch his body. (9) Despite such stand, Praneshacharya hesitates to advise the brahmins to perform the last rites, as Naranappa had smeared and sullied the brahminhood. He, therefore, suggests that a scriptural resolution to the crisis should be found.

Chandri at this moment surprises everybody by submitting all her gold ornaments to Praneshacharya for meeting out the expenses of Naranappa's last rites. This move startles the brahmins and their wives, bringing out their greed openly and coercing them to vehemently curse Naranappa. They recall how he was "hell-bent" on corrupting the young ones of the agrahara, inducing Garuda's son to run away and join the army, coaxing Lakshmana's son-in-law to spurn his family, killing off the sacred fish of the temple pond, inciting the young boys of Parijatapura to run after dramas and shows! (11) Praneshacharya anxiously thinks that "Chandri has spoiled everything with her good intentions." (10) During this conversation, the differences between the *Smartas* and the *Madhavas* are also hinted at, underlining the fact that equality is not fully practised within the same caste. Praneshacharya ultimately withdraws to seek a solution by referring to the scriptures. The question of who shall cremate Naranappa, and thereby possess the gold, is postponed for the night.

In the first chapter Anantha Murthy has vividly portrayed the character of Praneshacharya, the protagonist of the novel. His determination to lead an austere life, despite possessing minor paradoxes, wins him the respect of people. Anantha Murthy has also graphically presented the caricatures of other brahmins. Their eccentricities, greed, inner vacancy and the poor quality of their life is subtly suggested. The characterization of Chandri at this stage is rather sketchy. Anantha Murthy, though, is careful about taking the readers into his confidence. Hence, Chandri does not remain an altogether mute presence. She is careful about keeping the socially dictated norms, yet her compassion becomes palpable in her magnanimous gesture. Later incidents of the plot reinforce it significantly.

Chapter II

The daily routine of Praneshacharya, the spiritual leader of his community and the protagonist of the novel, and the barrenness of his personal life is treated in detail in the first chapter. The second chapter places him in the larger context of the community life, conveying simultaneously the absence of any transcending vision in the hackneyed routine of the brahmins. The imaginative stasis of the brahmin class and the consequential poverty of their life are dealt with a clarity of vision, which transforms the apparently simple chronicle into an allegorical representation of a group in a given social milieu.

The second chapter begins with a narration of the uniformity of the brahmin houses, both in their interiors and exteriors. The interiors are shorn of all luxuries, "cockroaches in the buttermilk shelves, fat rats in the store-room." (14) The middle-room has a rope stretched for a clothesline, marinated red peppers are spread out to dry on the verandah mat, and sacred balsam plants blossom in the backyard. The differences lie in the variety of the flowering trees in the backyard—*parijat*, jasmine, *champak*, *ranja* and *mandara* vie with each other. While the rest of the brahmins reserve their flowers for the worship of the Lord, Naranappa reserves the flowers of his backyard solely for the adornment of Chandri's hair. He also refuses to share his fruits with the other families. The chapter also depicts how the brahmins' lives run "smoothly" in "an annual cycle of appointments." (61) Their lives are ordered by rituals, festivals and seasonal variations of food. All twelve months of the year, the brahmins have different vows to keep, and they also wait for ritual feasts for death, marriage and initiation.

The readers are also told about the place-legends about the agrahara, Durvasapura. On a hillock, amidst the waters of the Tunga river, sage Durvasa is said to have performed his penance. It is also claimed that the Pandavas had lived at a short distance here for sometime, and Bhima had dammed up the Tunga river for Draupadi to swim. The dam was later broken at three different places—these three strands of water can be seen even now. The agrahara is thus famous for its legends, though they alone do not constitute its fame.

The agrahara is equally famous for its two brahmins, who have been presented as foils to each other. Praneshacharya, 'Crest-Jewel of Vedic Learning,' is a renowned ascetic. People from the neighbouring agraharas throng his place on special occasions to listen to his preachings. People also know about the misdeeds of the "scoundrel" Naranappa equally well: "So, the agrahara had become famous in all ten directions because of its legends, and also because of Praneshacharya . . . and certainly because of that scoundrel Naranappa. . . . Though Naranappa was a problem, the Acharya . . . bore up with Naranappa'a misdeeds. . . . His duties in this world grew lighter and more fragrant like sandalwood rubbed daily on stone." (17)

When Praneshacharya retires to consult the scriptures, the rest of the brahmins try to seek help from a neighbouring colony. They visit Manjayya in Parijatapura. The Brahmins of this locality are considered to be somewhat lower in social hierarchy. They mourn the death of Naranappa who was friendly with them, but panic at the idea of cremating his dead body as it may be treated as an unbrahminical act. They too decide to wait for Praneshacharya's counsel.

Chapter two presents a detailed background before the readers against which the plot develops. It is a "remarkable palimpsest of realistic details and allegorical nuances, setting the tone for the rest of the novel and highlighting its basic polarity between direct involvement in the sensuous aspects of life and a detachment through the denial of the senses."[3]

Chapter III

Praneshacharya reminiscences that Naranappa had always been a problematic presence in the village. In this chapter he recalls various confrontations he has had with Naranappa and concedes that the real challenge has been "to test which would finally win the Agrahara: his own penance and faith in ancient ways, or Naranappa's demoniac ways." (20) The Acharya had promised Naranappa's dying mother to bring her son back to right path. He fasts two nights in the week for him, but Naranappa persistently turns a deaf ear to his counsel. His evil influence has already resulted in the estrangement of two young brahmins, viz., Garuda's son Shyama and Lakshmana's son-in-law Shripati. Shyama has run away to join army, whereas Shripati has been ensnared by loose women.

Naranappa sneers at the Acharya and his brahmin ways. Claiming to belong to the "Hedonist School," he refuses to marry a relative, as is ordained by custom. He wants to roll up the brahmin respectability and "throw it always for a little bit of pleasure with one female." (21) He wants to open up the temple for all outcastes. He takes his Muslim friends to the Ganapati temple stream and catches the sacred free-swimming and trusting fish. When Acharya goes to meet him after this incident, he does not find any symptom of repentance in Naranappa's countenance. Laughingly he asks Chandri to serve liquor to the Acharya. He mocks at the Acharya's anger and discomfiture. He wants to destroy brahminism, but feels dejected as there is no actual brahmin really left to destroy in the agrahara—Praneshacharya being the only exception. He also castigates the evil practices of the other brahmins. He claims that the Acharya's recitation of erotic verses from Kalidasa roused the sensuous passion among the youngsters; and so he should be held responsible for corrupting the brahminism. He also jeers at the Acharya's puritan relationship with his wife, telling him to follow the examples of ancient sages who robustly enjoyed life, "Push those sickly wives of yours into the river. Be like the sages of your holy legends—get hold of a fish-scented fisherwoman . . . and go to sleep in her arms." (26) Praneshacharya is flabbergasted. Unable to grasp coherently Naranappa's comments, he is still appalled by them. He gives up telling the "luscious Puranic stories in the evenings" and starts on moral tales of penance. Consequently his listeners now comprise old dilapidated women, instead of bright-eyed young men. With such turbulent memories, he starts searching for the answer to his dilemma in the holy books.

This chapter significantly highlights the confusion Praneshacharya had felt in his relationship with Naranappa. Though he had staunchly stuck to his faith, he was unable to counter Naranappa's arguments. His decision to change the tone of his preaching can be treated as a gesture, without any polemics, to concede that the nature of truth depends on individual perspective.

Chapter IV

The fourth chapter describes how quotidian concerns become dominant in the absence of a transcendental vision. The avarice of the brahmins and their wives becomes apparent in the very beginning of the chapter. Garuda's son Shyama was incited by Naranappa to desert his family and join the army by signing a bond. Garuda's wife hopes that with the help of Chandri's jewellery they may be able to win their son's release. She sends her husband to the Acharya for pleading his case. Similarly, Lakshmana's wife considered Naranappa responsible for her son-in-law Shripati's desertion. She also holds him guilty for her sister's death. She also coaxes her husband to plead with the Acharya. Fed up with their bickering, the Acharya sends them away. After their departure he once again begins his studies. Despite several distractions, he does not forget to tend to his invalid wife. Constant reiteration of this fact underscores the Acharya's habitual action.

Chapter V

The minor character of Shripati is introduced in somewhat detail in this chapter. He was away for about a week, staying with a drama troupe, facilitating its performance in various ways. He was happy as the balladeer of the Kelur troupe, impressed by his pure enunciation and clear voice, had promised him a girl's role in next year's play. He hoped thus to escape the "brahmin dump" and its "endless funeral cakes and funeral porridge." (36) He was thus blissfully unaware of Naranappa's ailment and subsequent death.

Engrossed in his thoughts about Belli, his mistress and a minor character in the structure of the novel, and the pleasures awaiting him, he walks through the dark forest. Belli is a low-caste woman, and his paramour, "warm and ready—like a tuned-up drum." (37) No Brahmin girl could equal her as far as the sensuous participation of life. Shripati wistfully thinks of Naranappa and Chandri. He also thinks of Praneshacharya and his descriptions of beautiful women during his story-telling sessions. He considers the Acharya to be the best connoisseur of feminine charms and sympathizes with the celibate life he has to lead, "This man who speaks so beautifully about Kalidasa's women, does he feel any desire himself?" (39) He recalls how the Acharya's description of Shakuntala's beauty had excited him, and he was ravished by Balli's physical appeal when he saw her carrying a pitcher of water on her head in faded moonlight.

As he approaches the outcaste hutments on the hillside, he suddenly sees a hut on fire, burning away, silhouetted against the night sky. Later on he is told by Belli that a couple that day was "struck by a demon or something." Their bodies were left inside the hut and the hut was put on fire. She also tells him how rats and mice are coming out of their holes to die suddenly.

Shripati is suddenly anxious to see Naranappa. He finds the door unlatched, the house pervaded by a stench of something rotting. In the circle of his flashlight, he finds Naranappa's cold body on the floor, flies and small insects have infested it. Frightened by the horror of Naranappa's decayed body, he runs away in fear.

Chapter VI

Anantha Murthy has introduced several minor characters in *Samskara* to impart the much-needed local colour, and fill up the canvas of his story charmingly.

A macabre Dickensian character Lakshmidevamma is introduced in this chapter—an elderly lady habitual of nocturnal walks and bearing a grudge against Garudacharya. A child-widow, she is called Lakshmidevamma the Ill-Omen. After her relatives' death, Garudacharya's father had brought her to his house and taken the custody of whatever little property and jewellery she had possessed. Garuda's wife ill-treated her. Ultimately she was thrown out of their home, and forced to lead her life on the pittance of one rupee, Praneshacharya had persuaded Garuda to give her on a monthly basis. Her own misfortunes and Garuda's exploitation had turned her into a misanthrope. Unable to sleep peacefully, she walks down the streets at night and curses Garuda and his family. During one such night-walk she happens to look at Shripati rushing out of Naranappa's house. She takes it to be Naranappa's ghost and cries out in terror.

Chandri, who was lying on Praneshacharya's raised verandah, recognizes the running man as Shripati. Hunger has not allowed her to sleep; it drives her to the plantain grove, where she eats her fill. Her anxiety about Naranappa's proper burial is presented in detail. Though born to a family of prostitutes, she feels devoted to the man with whom she has spent ten years. Her behaviour and thinking patterns are moulded by traditional concerns. She does not want Naranappa to eat food cooked by her, but was unable to resist him. She is afraid that if not given a proper death-rite, he would surely become an evil spirit. She hopes that Praneshacharya is able to find out some remedy.

While Chandri sleeps on the verandah, Praneshacharya is busy in consulting the palm-leaf texts. He is afraid of admitting that the Book of Dharma has no solution to the present dilemma as it may lead to mockery by other pundits. The Acharya considers such possibility to be a personal defeat and wonders why he hadn't helped excommunicate Naranappa all these years. Naranappa's threat to turn Muslim in such case, coupled with the infinite compassion of the Acharya's heart had restricted the possibility of sucn an action. The Acharya wanted to bring him back to the right path.

Frustrated by his failure, the Acharya decides to go to the Maruti temple in the morning and seek divine guidance. Suddenly he remembers that Chandri is sleeping in the verandah without even a mat. He takes out a mat, a blanket and a pillow for her. As an afterthought he brings out the jewels she had surrendered earlier and returns them to her. He comments that Chandri's generosity has complicated the issue. It is a brahmin's duty to follow whatever is right for an emergency without any vacillation. Besides, Chandri may need her gold later.

The chapter highlights the Acharya's innate compassion for his fellow beings. His behaviour with his wife, Naranappa and Chandri is an evidence of his conviction that in a human being compassion is deeper rooted them desire.

Chapter VII

The banality and grotesqueness of the inner landscape is reinforced in this chapter by the annihilating stink of death which has enveloped the agrahara now. The brahmins and their family members are troubled by the stench of the rot. Rats are dying everywhere. Mothers keep the doors shut to prevent the children from going out into the street. Daily ritual of decorating the threshold with sacred designs and sprinkling of cowdung water in the yard cannot be performed because Naranappa's death rites have not been performed. "The agrahara didn't feel that morning had dawned yet. Things looked empty, desolate. . . . It felt as if there was a dead body in every house, in some dark room." (51) Children count the dying rats playfully. The brahmins try to pacify the fear generated by Lashmidevamma's cries of having seen Naranappa's ghost, and wait for Praneshacharya to bring back Maruti's divine decree.

Praneshacharya addresses his conflicts to the lord and leaves the decision on him, "If your orders are yes, give me the flower at your right, if you forbid the death-rite, give me the flower on the left." (54) Chandri waits outside the temple, pondering over her childless state, despite having spent ten years with Naranappa.

Chapter VIII

Unable to bear his hunger any more, Dasacharya decides to visit Manjayya's house at Parijatapura. He is afraid of asking openly for food, as Manjayya was a lowcaste Brahmin. After some small talk Manjayya invites him for a meal. Dasacharya depended on ritual meals for his livelihood. He is afraid that if people know about his acceptance of food in Manjayya's place, they may boycott him. Manjayya persuades him to take some milk and fruits. Later his wife also serves him some *uppittu*, happy to get an occasion to serve an upper-caste brahmin.

This chapter depicts traditional rigidity of the caste system and the consequential taboos people had to practice. The senselessness of such practices is also revealed, as also the social fear associated with them.

Chapter IX

Virginia Woolf, in her novel *The Years* (1937), had prologued each chapter by a description of nature which carried a weight of emotive associations and duplicated the tone of the rest of the chapter. Several chapters in *Samskara* too, follow a similar pattern. Chapter Nine opens with a small prosaic incident which subtly epitomizes the paltriness of life in the agrahara. Decay and death pervade it, as the brahmins wait for Praneshacharya to return from the Maruti temple. Yet there is no true expectation in their waiting, they seek only a relief in terms of performing the final rites of Naranappa.

Chinni has come to pick up the cowdung instead of Belli, whose parents are sick. She tells the women of the agrahara about the ailment which has gripped her own cluster of huts. Chinni cannot be given food directly in a plate as she is an untouchable. It can only be thrown to her from a distance. Acceptance of such practices with nonchalance though has a chilling effect on any contemporary reader. Incorporation of such subtle touches by Anantha Murthy outlines the caste prejudices prevalent in the rural India of the 1930s.

"Dissolved into formless anxiety" (59), the brahmins hung around waiting for the Acharya. Vultures come in hordes and settle down on rooftops, picking up the dying rats. Since these birds of prey are considered to be the harbingers of ill omen, people are afraid and try to shoo them away. It has no effect on the birds. Dasacharya suggests that gongs and conches may be used for driving the inauspicious, offensive birds away. This suggestion proves effective, but as soon as the brahmins stop beating the gongs and blowing their conches, vultures return. The starved brahmins soon feel exhausted. Their lassitude is reflected by the external surroundings too. There was not a breath of wind, "the stench stood stagnant in each house, and like a bodyless ghost it troubled everyone—wretched already with heat, hunger and dread." (61) The chapter clearly suggests the diabolic dimensions of devastation which echo the inner turbulence of mind.

Chapter X

This is the last chapter of Part I. It records Praneshacharya's rebirth. He patiently waits for some sign from the Maruti, at least for a flower to fall down, which could direct his actions regarding Naranappa's funeral. He waits throughout the day. When night falls, he remembers that it is time for his wife's medicine. Frustrated with his failure to get the right answer from Maruti, he stumbles out of the temple, helpless and sad. Chandri, who had been waiting outside, is overwhelmed by a tender compassion towards this brahmin who had perhaps never known the pleasures of woman. On the spur of the moment, the Acharya has a liaison with her. This encounter marks a turning point in his life. The complexities of Chandri's action are sacrificed to foreground the male sexual dilemma. The Maruti temple, where Praneshacharya worships, is dedicated to Hanuman, god of Chastity. By making love to Naranappa's mistress in its premises, he forfeits, in his own mind, the claim to guide the village spiritually. This incident also marks the beginning of the Acharya's wanderings to find out the truth about one's existence.

Part Two

Chapter I

Praneshacharya's encounter with Chandri is not merely a turning point in his life—it is a metaphorical rebirth that takes him "non-sequentially through life's stages beginning as a child."[4] It is midnight when he wakes up. He feels as if he has "fallen into his childhood, lying in his mother's lap and finding rest there after great fatigue." (67) With a changed and renewed perspective, he experiences the world. He smells the fragrant grass, wet earth, wild flowers and looks at the sacred constellation with a sense of novelty. His ethical consciousness though has not deserted him. He tells Chandri that he has lost the authority to take any decisions for the agrahara and is ready to perform the funeral rites himself. (68)

Chandri has slight remorse at the complexities she had unwittingly generated—first by offering her gold, then by offering herself. Unaccustomed to self-reproach as she is, she overcomes such feelings easily and decides to go to Naranappa's home. She finds that the body has swollen and become disfigured. She cannot associate the bloated body with the man she had loved. Afraid, she runs to cartman Sheshappa's house and requests him to cremate Naranappa. Sheshappa panics at the thought of meddling with a brahmin corpse. Chandri is baffled. She is convinced that after death Naranappa's body is neither brahmin, nor shudra. It is simply a carcass, "a stinking rotting carcass." (70) She goes to the Muslim section of the village and offers money to Ahmad Bari, the fish merchant. Ahmad remembers Naranappa's kindness, who had once loaned him money to buy oxen when he was bankrupt. He secretly loads the body and the firewood in his bullock-cart, drives to the cremation ground and kindles a flapping flaming fire. Afterwards, Chandri comes back home, collects a few silk saris in a bag, bundles up the cash and the gold ornaments the Acharya had returned and walks into the forest, planning to catch the morning bus to Kundapura, a neighbouring town from where she had initially come.

Chandri's character reveals a rare sensitivity, rather dormant, owing to the overwhelming social pressures and limitations. She does not understand religious intricacies, but decides to act under an intuitive determination to cremate the body of a person she had lived with for ten years.

Chapter II

This chapter brings with it a comic relief with its portrayal of a drama troupe. Several young men from different agraharas have gathered round a harmonium donated by Naranappa to rehearse a play. Naranappa was the prime motivator for the formation and continued activities of the Parijata Drama Group. Descriptions of the chapter display hitherto hidden facets of his character. He comes across as a gregarious person, a nonconformist at heart, ready to experiment with new ideas. His admission of belonging to the hedonist school is authenticated by the description of this chapter.

After the rehearsal is over, five close friends of Naranappa decide to secretly cremate his body. In drunken stupor they reach his house, but find it totally empty. Chandri had already taken away the corpse and cremated it. The young men from the troupe are afraid for their lives. Thinking that Naranappa has turned into a ghost, they run away. Half-wit Lakshmidevamma sees them in the darkness, running helter-skelter, and shrieks in fear.

Chapter III

The agrahara passes the night restively. "In house after house, children, mother and father seemed to become one shapeless mass, hugging each other and shivering in the dark." (74)

Vultures return again in the morning and brahmins try to shoo them away by beating the gongs. Praneshacharya is baffled when he hears these auspicious sounds. Having spent the previous day at the Maruti temple, he was unaware of the menace of vultures. Also, his encounter with Chandri has changed his perspective. While attending to his wife's needs, he for the first time looks at her as a woman and is appalled by the ugliness of her body. The long-practised routine of doctor-patient relations, of indifferent affection and compassion is severed suddenly. He feels that he had lost hold of the rites and actions he had clutched at till now.

Praneshacharya was married early; he was sixteen at the time of his marriage. Leaving his invalid wife at her parental house, he had gone to Benares for higher studies and later became the 'Crest-Jewel of Vedanta Philosophy.' He treated his marital life as a test of his non-attachment. His encounter with Chandri upturns his world. He realizes that he had never treated beauty as an object of desire, the way he had read about in the classics.

For the first time in his life too, he has an urge to tell a lie to hide things for one's own welfare. In Chandri's absence, he is unable to admit the truth before the congregation of brahmins. He simply conveys his failure to get any direction from Maruti, and asks them to do whatever their hearts say. The disappointed brahmins decide to go to Pundit Subbannacharya at Kaimara agrahara. From there, they also plan to visit their spiritual guru. They also decide to send their families to their in-laws' places. The Acharya feels relieved.

The passivity of the Brahmins can be palpably discerned in their desire to seek guidance from other agencies. Their lack of initiative, dependence on customs, and an inner fear of committing anything sacrilegious inadvertently have gripped their conscience and nibbled at their capacity of freethinking.

Chapter IV

By the time the brahmins are ready to leave, Praneshacharya's wife has started her period. Unable to leave her alone, he stays back in the village. The rest of the brahmins reach the Kaimara agrahara, where they bathe, eat and rest. The pundit shows his inability to guide them, but declares Naranappa's death to be a malignant one. Next morning when the brahmins ready themselves for the journey, they find that Dasacharya is suffering from fever. Padmanabhacharya also develops high fever en route. The death toll has begun.

Chapter V

A terrible leery silence settles on the agrahara once the brahmins go away. The dreary tone of the description of this chapter underscores the banality and grotesqueness of the situation.

Praneshacharya was alone with his ill wife. His loneliness is accentuated by the absence of sacrosanct noises associated with the rituals of daily worship. He feels acutely disturbed by the continuous presence of a rotting stench, raucous cries of vultures and crows, and dying rats. Unable to bear it any longer, he crosses the stream and eats some plantains under the shade of a tree. He remembers Chandri and is aware of his own body's tigerish lust, tamed thus far by an imposed righteousness. He also recalls Naranappa's mocking exhortations. He realizes that before his experience with Chandri he had not actually lived, but was going through repetitive motions perfected by habit. His boyhood sensations have returned to him now to complete the process of his rebirth. He recalls his unsophisticated boyhood desires, goes back to the place of his amorous meeting with Chandri. Absence of any activity soothes him. He smells grass blades, "just sitting coolly under a tree had become a fulfillment, a value." (83) He is now able to gratefully receive the pleasures of living, putting aside both desire and value.

After having spent some pleasant moments of inactivity in the forest, the Acharya returns to the agrahara, remembering that it was time to give his wife her gruel. He finds her flushed with high fever. By evening she is dead. Praneshacharya walks to Kaimara in the dead of the night. As he enters Subbannacharya's home, he happens to meet four brahmins who are returning after the cremation of Dasacharya. With their help he cremates his wife.

Chapter VI

The brahmins who had gathered at the monastery, remain silent till the holy feast is over. Afterwards they share their plight with the guru. The guru unequivocally tells them that though Naranappa gave up brahminism, brahminism cannot leave him. He suggests that he should be duly cremated, and to clear the impurities of his life all his property must be offered to the monastery. The attempts of Garudacharya and Lakshmanacharya to register a protest against his decree are brushed away perfunctorily. Garudacharya is running temperature and is left behind by the rest of the brahmins who are now in a hurry to finish the funeral rites of Naranappa.

Praneshacharya does not return to the agrahara after his wife's cremation. Shunning all worldly possessions, taking nothing with him, he moves out on an unknown path of self-discovery.

Part III

Chapter I

Brahminism in India is not simply a distinction based on mere professional practices; it is a specific way of understanding the external and internal worlds. It can be termed as a way of life, a preference for attitudes which comprehensively pervades different facets of a man's life; conscious, as well as subconscious. Praneshacharya had lived his life till this juncture according to the tenets of brahminism, so far he had led a conditioned life within a pre-defined milieu. After his encounter with Chandri he feels that he has been cut off from this world of certainties and possesses no moral obligation/right to guide the brahmins of the agrahara. He is suddenly freed from the traditional limitations of the caste and decides to walk into the forest and travel wherever his legs will take him. He "walks away free, leaving everything behind" (91), with neither duties, nor debts. Anantha Murthy delineates the complexity and ambiguity of one's quest for self-identification through his character. Shorn of the burden of choosing the right path of action, he wants to lead a life without desire. He questions his past actions, and is eager to find a definite pattern for his wanderings. Soon he is tired and sits under a tree on the edge of a village.

At this moment, an ordinary farmer approaches him. He treats the Acharya like an ordinary brahmin who is going for his collection. The Acharya is initially disturbed by such behaviour, but soon regains his composure. He realizes that his caste shall always cling to him when the farmer asks to perform some routine brahmin functions (96). In his turbulent frame of mind, he is also afraid of meeting an acquaintance. He repents the loss of his original fearlessness. His difference and consequential inability to live in full view of the other brahmins forces him to wander further. His search for a new form has begun. He has lost the past form, but has not found the new one, his present state is like a "demoniac premature foetus taken hastily out of the womb." (98) He realizes at this juncture that the destiny of an individual is shaped through his own choices.

Praneshacharya reminiscences about his student life. He particularly recalls his friend Mahabala, who had accompanied him to Kashi for higher studies, and for whom he had a terrible jealousy; strangely, also a terrible love (99). Mahabala wanted to seek the truth; for him God was a passionate hunger. But gradually he gave up his studies and started to live with a prostitute. Praneshacharya had vowed never to follow that route. It was to make up for his defeat in Mahabala's case that he wanted to mould Naranappa according to his own preferences. Here, too, he had failed. Engrossed in his thoughts, he walks deeper into the forest. Suddenly he becomes aware of the presence of another human being, shadowing him continuously. It turns out to be Putta, a villager, who is going for the car-festival at Melige. The Acharya does not want to talk to him but he sticks to him and becomes his constant companion till the very end of the novel.

Chapter II

Soon after the departure of the Acharya, people of Parijatapura come to know everything, except that Naranappa's body was cremated by a Muslim. Disturbed by the series of deaths Manjayya fears an epidemic and decides to inform the municipal authorities about it. The brahmins also return from the monastery and find Padmanabhacharya lying in a coma. Dasacharya and Garudacharya are also sick. They also come to know about the death of the Acharya's wife. They are bewildered by the sudden overwhelming confusion which has gripped their familiar world. Unaware that Naranappa's body has already been cremated they are reluctant to perform the rites of an already decomposed body. However, pressures of day-to-day life and the compulsion of looking after the cows drive them towards it. They go back to the agrahara, muttering God's name meanwhile. Belli's parents also die and she runs away from the village.

Meanwhile, Putta accompanies Praneshacharya in his wanderings. Treating the Acharya as a common mendicant brahmin on his beggarly rounds, he advises him on worldly matters. The Acharya does not want to befriend him, but Putta sticks to him, changing even his programmes to suit the Acharya's desire. Eventually they reach Melige, a small town which is holding a festival. Putta accompanies him to various shops. The colourful gaiety affects the Acharya strangely—the smell of new clothes, the song of the balloon-seller, the sights of the Bombay Box, the acrobat show convince him that till this point he had stood outside the world of ordinary pleasures. When Putta invites him to a coffee shop, he is initially afraid of being seen by some acquaintance. He, though, immediately resolves to rid himself of such fears (115). Troubled by a sense of fate he realizes that he would never have the courage to defy brahmin practices as Naranappa had done (116). While witnessing the cockfight he feels that he has been abruptly dropped in a demonic world. He is perplexed as he does not have the necessary "skills to live in this world of sharp and cruel feelings." (117) It was a "demon world of pressing need, revenge, greed" and he was like a "futile ghost" (120), witnessing it from a peripheral position, afraid of being dragged into the main arena.

Putta ultimately brings the Acharya to Padmavati's house. She is a half-caste Malera woman, who strongly exudes an earthly sensuality. The Acharya feels the vague stirrings of desire in him. He is also bewildered by the various facets of his personality he had to exhibit within the course of a single day. Within a single day, he had become many persons. The Acharya realizes that "in the eyes of the strangers, one gets a new form." (123) He decides to leave this ghostly stage behind and to search out his roots. Leaving Padmavati's house, he goes to the temple for dinner. Recognized by a man while taking his meals, he suddenly leaves the temple premises. However, he soon overcomes his diffidence, and decides to speak the truth to his fellow brahmins. He realizes that "only the form we forge for ourselves in our inmost will is ours without question." (135) He decides to get back to Durvasapura immediately. Putta also decides to accompany him, as he wanted to negotiate the purchase of an orchard with Naranappa. The Acharya does not disclose his true identity to Putta even now. He also does not tell him about Naranappa's death. The novel ends with the beginning of the Acharya's return journey to the agrahara. He is a different person now. Freed from the traditional brahministic rituals, he has tasted the sensuousness of his early youth, and has determined now to initiate a new phase of his life, based on a frank admission of his actions. During his journey—literal as well as metaphorical—he has accepted the presence of several doubts and questions in his mind. The questions still remain unanswered. Anantha Murthy has desisted from making any authorial decision. Rather, he has shifted the choice of taking an ethical judgement on the readers. In his note, A.K. Ramanujan has rightly pointed out that the novel suggests a movement, not a closure, "The novel ends, but does not conclude." (147)

NOTES

1. A.K. Ramanujan, translator's note, *Samskara*, U.R. Anantha Murthy (New Delhi: Oxford University Press, 1978), p. 141.
2. Meenakshi Mukherjee, "*Samskara*," Baral et al, ed., *U.R. Anantha Murthy's "Samskara": A Critical Reader* (New Delhi: Pencraft, 2005), p. 83.
3. Christian Fornalel, http: //www3.haverford.edu/relg/sells/ courses/ rel101/ P_VsysteminSamskara.com
4. Meenakshi Mukherjee, p. 86.

Caste as Character in *Samskara*

RASHMI GAUR

The word *caste* etymologically belongs to the Portuguese language. It means breed or race. In Sanskrit language, the equivalent word is *varna*, which changes its meaning according to the context in which it is used and can denote form, quality, class, category, race, merit or virtue. The caste system is very intricate and complicated, and often generates sweeping generalizations. Parallel can be seen with the European system of guilds that divided artisans into separate social and economic entities on the basis of their specialization and sub-specializations.[1] The system must have developed out of necessity as a stratified and hierarchical socio-economic order to absorb different people within a homogeneous social structure. Eventually, however, it came to signify "an endogamic group, its members linked by heredity, marriage, custom and profession."[2] Whole groups of people must have taken on a new identity which was associated with the economic activity of their *gotra* (clan). The social practices governing the rigidity of the caste system, and the taboos against inter-caste marriages and free mixing soon degenerated into an inflexible hierarchical structure of social inequality in which one's rank is ascribed at birth and little mobility is allowed out of the position to which a person is born. It has thus damaged human progress and abetted suffering. An important aspect of Hindu social structure, it has been portrayed in various works of fiction. In *Samskara* too, its intriguing complexities are subtly woven in the thematic motifs.

The caste system is based upon the organization of society in four distinct classes, traditionally known as *chaturvarna*. The origin of this division can be found in *Purusha Sukta*, the Ninetieth Hymn of the Tenth *Mandala* of the *Rig Veda*. The *Purusha Sukta* is a theory of the origin of the universe, a cosmogony. The

Egyptians also had an elaborate theory about it. Another similar cosmogony is found in Chapter 1 of the Genesis in the *Old Testament*. Cosmogonies have never been more than matters of academic interest. This is true of some parts of the *Purusha Sukta*, but not of the whole of it: verses 11 and 12 fall in one category and the rest of the verses fall in another. Verses other than 11 and 12 are not in common circulation. Verses 11 and 12 contain the origin and classification of castes. A centuries old tradition treats them as containing a mandatory injunction from the creator to the effect that society must be constituted on the basis of four classes mentioned in the *Sukta*. These verses contain a divine injunction prescribing a particular form of the constitution of society.[3]

It is said that there are four castes—Brahmins, Kshatriyas, Vaishyas and Shudras. Among these, each preceding caste is superior by birth to the one following. *Purusha* is said to be a symbol of the universe, immortal and supreme, who has been given human attributes. It is said that the Brahmin was his mouth, the Kshatriya formed his arms, the Vaishya his thighs and the Shudra was born from his feet. This theory was later on incorporated in other religious texts, including the *Apastamba Dharma Sutra*, *Vashishtha Dharma Sutra*, the *Vishnu Purana*, the *Harivansha*, the *Satpatha Brahmin* and the *Manu Smriti* etc.[4] Alan Dundes, a Professor of Anthropology and Folklore at the University of California at Berkeley, has offered a Freudian analysis of caste and untouchability in his book *Two Tales of Sparrow and Crow* (Rowman Littlefield, 1997). He says that it is the persistent, obsessive fear that the top, clean mouth might be contaminated or defiled from the bottom that "underlies and permeates the entire caste system. This explains why a higher caste cannot accept food from the hands of a lower caste . . . feet are dirty because they are in contact with the outside ground where faeces might lurk."[5]

U.R. Anantha Murthy's novel *Samskara* traces several contemporary social practices—conscious as well as unconscious—and discusses how in daily life caste becomes the basis of labour division, social discrimination and gender exploitation. The novel begins with the death of Naranappa by bubonic plague. In his life he had violated all the taboos propagated and fostered by the brahminic culture of the agrahara. The brahmins face the dilemma of conducting his last rites without inviting social ostracism and wait for the decision of Praneshacharya in this regard. Praneshacharya, the protagonist of the novel, is the spiritual guide of the agrahara brahmins. Initially it is his ascetic brahmin identity, which is introduced to the readers. But he also possesses greater "kindness, sensitivity and tolerance of human failing, traits which lead him to an empathy (and consequent sexual intercourse) with Naranappa's mistress, the prostitute Chandri."[6] Praneshacharya's sketch, and also other discourses which inform us of action, underline the disastrous dimensions of the caste calculus in the agrahara.

The concept of the caste which has crystallized in the Indian social structure was made doubly rigorous by integrating it with religion. The cyclical theory of rebirth, with the possibility of birth in a higher caste being linked to faithfully carrying out one's duties as per caste rules generated a fatalistic acceptance of one's situation. The pseudo-religious practices of untouchability and endogamy which segregated one caste from another, apart from the various social privileges, drilled into the minds of people that caste is a preordained and hereditary institution which has divine sanction. *Samskara* indicates the relationship between the division of labour and caste. Brahmins were originally the people who preached spiritual teachings to the society and lived ascetic spiritual lives. The *Mahabharata* defines a brahmin as one who is truthful, forgiving and kind. Praneshacharya possesses these qualities and devotedly practises his religious duties. 'Crest-Jewel of Vedic Learning,' he visits the Maruti temple daily for worship. The brahmins of the agrahara assemble at his place daily to listen to his recitation of sacred legends (1). In all religious matters, he is the ultimate arbiter. People look up to him for guidance and consolation. The brahmin wives ask their husbands to wait till he has reached a decision about Naranappa's last rites (4). He embodies the virtuous facets of traditional Brahmin cult with its emphasis on learning, asceticism and compassion. Even Naranappa has to accept it grudgingly, "my only sorrow is that there's no brahminism left to destroy in this place—except you." (23) Looking at him Chandri recalls her mother who used to say that prostitutes should get pregnant by such holy men, "he had such looks, virtues; he glowed. But one had to be lucky to be blessed by such people." (46) When Chandri and Praneshacharya together return from the Maruti temple, she is conscious of the "great good fortune that had suddenly rushed into her life." (68)

Traditionally brahmins depended on performing religious rituals for their livelihood. Absence of any other skill often resulted in acute poverty in a world which was shifting towards major changes in its socio-economic views and practices. *Samskara* graphically portrays the constrictions of a caste based economic choice. Brahmins of the agrahara are poor and ill fed. Lakshamancharya is depicted as having "sunken cheeks, yellow eyes deep in sockets, ribs protruding . . . altogether an unbalanced body." (4). Dasacharya lived "entirely on the meals that brahmins get at death-rites and anniversaries." (8). Untrained in any alternate skill, hesitant to accept new ways, these Brahmins are as much a victim of the caste system as the lower castes. Their blinkered vision smothers the spontaneity of their life.

The listless poverty of the brahmins of the agrahara is presented in the novel through various episodes. They depended on cucumber during the rainy season for everything, "curry, mash, or soup made with the seeds." (16) They could walk a distance of thirty miles just for attending a festival feast. Comparing Belli with other Brahmin girls, Shripati scathingly remarks, "cheek sunken, breast withered, mouth stinking of lentil soup." (37) Such incidents describe the poverty of the brahmins, who are traditionally linked with professional choices and cannot escape them. When Praneshacharya takes up wandering, he is approached by a villager who requests him to read "a bit of the future." (95) Praneshacharya was about to perform the routine brahmin functions by sheer habit, when he reins himself suddenly and ruefully ponders that one cannot run away from one's caste, "Even if I leave everything behind, the community clings to me, asking me to fulfill duties the brahmin is born to." (96) The inescapability of the caste is discernible in the debate which followed Naranappa's death. He had violated and profaned all codes of conduct, still he could not be treated as an outcaste and "remains a Brahmin in his death." (9)

Another aspect of caste based discrimination which *Samskara* presents before us is related with the taboos.which prohibit a brahmin to eat food touched/prepared by a member of a different caste. Religious treatises like the *Vashishtha Dharma Sutra* specify what may be eaten and what may not. It stipulates that a Brahmin cannot eat food given by a shudra. The caste system accepts and encourages a rigid hierarchical structure of social inequality—the greater one's purity, or lack of contact with pollution, the higher one's rank is. Dasacharya is afraid of social criticism, if he openly eats food at Manjayya's place. Being a *smarta*, Manjayya is considered to belong to a lower sect of brahmins. Dasacharya is afraid that if he eats "cooked stuff in a *Smarta* house" (57), he may be socially boycotted by his own sect, "I don't really mind eating in your house. But if those rascals in our agrahara hear about it, no one will invite me to a ceremony again. What can I do, Manjayya?" When Manjayya amusedly assures him of secrecy, Dasacharya asks for some milk, jaggery and plain flat-rice. Secretly delighted that an agrahara Brahmin had come to eat with them, his wife gleefully serves him. Naranappa did not practise such discrimination, yet Chandri was unable to come to terms with his unorthodox behaviour. She repeatedly requests him not to eat food cooked by her (45). Society can perhaps pardon Naranappa for having close relationship with a lowcaste prostitute, but the fact that he ate what Chandri cooked is still graver; Lakshmana's statement, in which he lays emphasis on the fact that he, in addition to having a mistress, even ate food cooked by her, makes it amply clear.

Contact with a person of a lower caste can negatively alter one's purity and may require some form of remedial procedure, such as bathing or changing clothes. When Chandri calls at Praneshacharya's home to inform him about Naranappa's death, he had yet to take his meal. The readers are told how he will have to bathe again to purify himself if he talks to Chandri before taking his food, "If the Acharya talked to her, he would be polluted; he would have to bathe again before his meal." (2) Being a traditional Brahmin, Praneshacharya has been conditioned not to eat food cooked or served by a person who belongs to a lower caste. It is a commonly followed practice as other people also know and respect this constraint. Putta takes the Acharya to a brahmin restaurant for a coffee, telling him that they keep a special place inside for orthodox brahmins like him. Still fearing the presence of some familiar person, the Acharya is worried as it may have a ripple effect later on, "If someone sees the crest Jewel of Vedanta Philosophy drinking a cup of polluted restaurant coffee." (115) Afraid of entering a temple and eating there during the period of his wife's mourning, he realizes that he would never have the courage to defy Brahmin practices as Naranappa had done (116). Many anthropologists have remarked on the critical importance of pollution to the caste system. A non-brahmin, particularly a shudra, an untouchable, is never considered clean enough either to share food with the brahmin, or even to touch him. When Chandri requests Sheshappa, the cartman, to cremate Naranappa's body, he refuses, "Chandravva, that can't be done. Do you want me to go to hell, meddling with a brahmin corpse? Even if you give me all eight kinds of riches, I can't." (69-70) The internalization of caste hierarchy can also be seen in Putta's attempts to climb the caste ladder by denying the social background of his mother. He tells Praneshacharya that he is a Malera; though his mother belonged to a lower caste and was not married to his father who was a high-class Brahmin. He flaunts the scared thread and claims that all his buddies are Brahmin boys (112).

Samskara presents a vivid picture of a society which has accepted caste discrimination as a norm. It has unquestioningly accepted the brahmin eminence, and pushed the lower-caste people to a periphery. Brahmins are supposed to be the spiritual and temporal guides, teachers and exponents of law, whereas the shudras perform menial services only. They are routinely denied even the semblance of equality. Their hutments are quite a distance away from the brahmin agrahara (39). The abject poverty of their life is also discernible. They depend on manual labour for their livelihood. Chinni and Belli pick up the cow dung. They are treated with indifference. Chinni begs for something to eat, standing at a distance from a brahmin woman, "Please, *avva*, throw a morsel for my mouth, *avva*." (58) Betel leaf, betel nut and tobacco are thrown at her from some distance. Such incidents highlight the extent of untouchability practised in the contemporary South Indian society.

Thus we see that the caste emerges as an independent character in *Samskara*. It informs the action, moulds the characters' responses and also provides the much-needed sociological background.

NOTES

1. Terence Callaham and Roxanna Pavich, "Indian Caste System," http://www.csuchico.edu/-cheinz/syllabi/asst001/spring98/india.htm.
2. *Ibid.*
3. http;//www.ambedkar.org/ambcd/3881%wh%20th%20Sudhras%20PART%20I.htm
4. *Ibid.*
5. http://www.scienceblog.com/community.
6. Nalini Natarajan, "Gender and Caste: Modernity in U.R. Anantha Murthy's *Samskara*" Baral, Rao and Rath, *U.R. Anantha Murthy's Samskara: A Critical Reader* (Delhi: Pencraft, 2005), p. 152.
7. http;//www.ambedkar.org/ambcd/3881%wh%20th%20Sudhras%20PART%20I.htm.

Construction of Gender: Women Characters in *Samskara*

RASHMI GAUR

Individual cognition of gender is often influenced and conditioned by one's perception of social stereotypes, and therefore may not remain agentic. Whereas sexual differences are biological and fixed, the notion of gender is a variable constructed by the society. Feminist critics have argued that the "true woman" is an "artificial product that civilization makes, as formerly eunuchs were made."[1] The social concept of feminine docility mutilates the assertiveness of women and goads them to seek their fulfillment through domesticity or through others. The social structures of a society, which also control systems of power, impart a particular shape to the concept of gender. "People are made into social men and women by the particular positions which they are allocated in the social order. To understand what it is to be a man or woman in a given society is to grasp the social relations involved."[2] In patriarchal set-ups, gender divisions are exploitative and oppressive for women. They are treated as subordinate to men. Individual and social understanding of gender notions is reflected in literary texts through characters, plot development, imagery, symbolism and language practices. *Samskara* too is not an exception. It poignantly illustrates the indoctrination of centuries, as far as the role and status of women are concerned, against a rural South Indian backdrop. It also shows how this society endeavours to stifle the individuality of women in a gradual but planned way, and encourages men to be insensitive towards it.

Samskara presents the life ot a brahmin agrahara through its protagonist, Praneshacharya. The descriptions are not only replete with local trappings, they also reverberate with an inner continuation of traditional attitudes towards women. The novel transparently displays the novelist's unquestioned acceptance of the prevalent notions about gender roles; the desire to penetrate deeper into the psyche of women is conspicuously absent. A closer study of the women characters of the novel underscores this point.

Women characters primarily appear in two contexts in the novel, namely the economic and the sexual.[3] The novel repeatedly refers to the brahmin women's greed and their lust for gold. When Chandri offers her ornaments for meeting out the expenses of Naranappa's death rites, the brahmin women are mesmerized, "The women calculated swiftly; that heap of gold was worth at least two thousand rupees. One after another the wives scanned the husbands' faces." (10) Again, the brahmins' internal bickering and indecisiveness infuriates them, "The women kept staring at the heap of gold and they were disappointed by their husbands' words." (12) Garuda's wife Sitadevi and Lakshmana's wife Anasuya persuade their husbands to visit Praneshacharya to plead their cases (28-33).

Women of the agrahara are also denied the acknowledgement of their daily labour in performing the household chores. Wherever such activities are mentioned, specific reference to women has not been made. Decorating the threshold, sprinkling of cowdung water in the courtyard, preparation of food, preserving vegetables for the rainy season, washing of the clothes and disciplining the children are some domestic activities which the narrative clearly links with women. Yet they are never illustrated as active agents. Their presence is peripheral, though the life of the agrahara depends on their labour for smooth functioning. They cajole their children to remain inside to avoid the overwhelming stench (51), prepare food (52), preserve cucumbers for the rainy season (16), ritually wash saris (14); however, the performance of all such duties is taken for granted and is not equated with any positive contribution.

Samskara also highlights the superstitious attitudes against women, perpetuated by social customs. Praneshacharya cannot shift his wife when the rest of the brahmins decide to send away their families to their in-laws, as she had started her period (80). Abhorrence for impurities, conventionally associated with the bodily functions of women, is a belief cherished in all patriarchal set-ups, which systematically nurtures a consciousness of their secondary status among women. Praneshacharya, seeped into the values of traditional brahminic culture, unquestioningly accepts such values. Disturbed by the eerie silence of the agrahara and the pervading stench, he had taken refuge in the forest which was still resonant with the memories of Chandri. Towards the evening when he returns to the agrahara, he finds that his invalid wife is flushed with fever. He hesitates before checking her temperature, "How can I touch a woman polluted by her menstrual blood." (84) Nalini Natrarajan in her notes has commented on the untouchability of women during their menstrual cycle.[4] Remembering the stories from scriptures Praneshacharya used to narrate, Shripati vividly remembers a description, "Like the thighs of a blossoming woman, pure after her monthly baths." (38) Tradition encourages men to treat women only as sex objects.

Brahmin women live in the background. Not only their household chores have been mentioned independent of any association with their labour, they are invariably portrayed occupying the periphery after having surrendered the centrestage to their men. With meek silence they listen to the lengthy discussions about Naranappa's burial. Stunned by Chandri's generosity of surrendering her ornaments, they gaze at their husbands' faces. When Anasuya, Lakshmana's wife, blurts out her anger with snide comments and sobs, she is conveniently ignored. They are mute listeners, forbidden by custom to be direct participants in any decision making process. Among other talks, they also listen to the frivolous licenses their husbands and their ancestors have had with lowcaste women and prostitutes. Durgabhatta cackles about how the ancient sages had cohabited with Dravidian women (6), Garudacharya quotes the folklore about Shankaracharya occupying the dead body of a king for gaining fuller experience of life (6-7), Lakshmana talks about Naranappa enjoying food cooked by Chandri, a lowcaste prostitute and his mistress (6), Praneshacharya narrates the erotic stories from the religious texts (24). Women, however, never have a direct participation in dialogue. Their conditioned sensitivity is being used as a tool to further the patriarchal order and to ensure the continuity of their servility.

Anantha Murthy's description of Brahmin women in the *Samskara* repeatedly stresses their lack of sexuality. He highlights their traditional, socially defined and pre-fixed roles only. Unequivocal denial of sexual exuberance to brahmin women somehow mitigates their autonomous identity, acting simultaneously as an abetting factor for their husband's infidelity. Their lack of sexual charm is offered almost as an excuse for Naranappa's and Sripati's desertion of their wives. Naranappa and others frequently refer to the folklore of *matsyagandha* (23). Naranappa goes to the extent of advising Praneshacharya to "push those sickly wives of yours into the river. Be like the sages of your holy legends—get hold of a fish—scented fisherwoman." (26) Shripati is equally vocal, "which brahmin girl—cheek sunken, breast withered, mouth stinking of lentil soup—which Brahmin girl was equal to Belli?" (37) His own wife Lilavati has been described as "short, plump and round, a nose-ring in, one nostril. . . . Wearing a dwarfish braid of hair very tight." (31) Even her mother's heart hardens whenever she looks at her. Her constant denial to impart conjugal bliss to her husband drives him towards Belli.

The illustrations of the brahmin women in *Samskara* clearly evince how gender formation is organically linked with the concept of caste within Indian social milieu. Patriarchal norms become doubly rigid within the stratification of caste. Traditional marriages can take place only within the same caste; there are also rigid laws governing the partaking of food with members of other groups. Similarly, each caste has its taboos as far as the behavioural norms of women are concerned. The inviolability of taboos is relaxed for men, as is evident in the case of Naranappa. Despite his flagrant repudiation of social norms, the agrahara brahmins are unable to excommunicate him, "he may have rejected Brahminhood, but brahminhood never left him. No one ever excommunicated him officially." (9)

In stark.contrast to the shrivelled sensuality of the brahmin women, *Samskara* portrays women like Chandri and Belli, who belong to lower castes and almost flaunt their exuberant sexuality. They have been depicted as possessing a vigorous sensuality and prefer a direct participation in life. The relaxed constrictions about their movements are related with the norms of their caste. They are depicted as temptresses, the text suggests that the brahmin men cannot escape their lure. In another perspective it can be suggested that the lower-caste women are treated merely as sex objects. Within the framework of Indian caste system, feminine problems cannot be comprehensively represented. It is sometimes perceived that the freedom of movement traditionally extended to the lower caste women is synonymous with autonomous self-hood. Such generalization ignores the socio-cultural realities became such women cannot choose to be otherwise. Their relatively free movements and compulsions of physical labour do not liberate them; they only indicate their economic, class and gender oppression. The absence of sexual taboos in their life does not constitute a choice, it only facilitates their exploitation by the upper caste male. In *Samskara* too, the socio-economic reasons of their victimization are glossed over and the brahmin men's transgression to satisfy their casual carnal desires are accepted as norms. *Samskara* repeatedly refers to the folklore: ancestors cohabiting with Dravidian women, the legend of the *matsyagandha*, people visiting the brothels of Basrur in South Kanara, the story of the *Shakuntalam*. Returning from Shrinali, Shripati pleasantly anticipates his rendezvous with Belli (37). Naranappa mockingly tells Praneshacharya, "who in the world can live with a girl who gives no pleasure—except of course some barren Brahmins." (21) Praneshacharya longingly hankers for Chandri's presence, "He had not so far desired any of the beauty he'd read about in the classics. . . . Now he wanted for himself a share of all that." (77) Such descriptions augment the fact that gendered identities are a consequence of one's initiation into a particular culture, and its mores of defining social relationships.

Samskara introduces various female characters to us. However, the only woman character which has been developed fully is that of Chandri. She can be termed as a round character. E.M. Forster has remarked that the test of a round character is whether it is capable of surprising the readers in a convincing way. A round character must have the incalculability of life within the pages of a book.[5] Chandri possesses the profundities and complexities of the human mind, and develops with changing circumstances. Her portrayal also indicates her readiness for an "extended life."[6]

Chandri is introduced to us right in the beginning of the novel as Naranappa's concubine (2) and a lowborn prostitute (5). Praneshacharya is aware that he would be polluted after talking to her. She is shunned by the brahmins of the agrahara, even though Naranappa always treated her with a sense of equality, even eating the food cooked by her (6). Chandri does not possess any cultural talent. Rather, she has ungrudgingly accepted her secondary social status and learnt to act accordingly. When she goes to Praneshacharya to inform him about Naranappa's death, she stands meekly in the yard (2). She also requests Naranappa not to eat food cooked by her (45). While the brahmins gather to discuss the matter of Naranappa's rites, she remains on the periphery, sitting against a pillar (7). Her spontaneous decision to offer her gold for the expenses of the rites startles everyone. "Suddenly Chandri did something that stunned the brahmins. She moved forward to stand in the front courtyard. . . . Loosened her four-strand gold chain, her thick bracelet, her bangles, and placed them all in a heap before Praneshacharya. She mumbled something about all this jewellery being there for the expenses of the rite, and went back to stand in her place." (9-10)

Chandri's sensitivity can be discerned in her concern for Naranappa's last rites. She is afraid that if he is not cremated properly, he may turn into an evil spirit. She is determined not to let it happen, "She'd eaten his salt, she, Chandri." (45-46) Sitting on the verandah, waiting for Praneshacharya's decision, she even tries to push her drowsiness away (46). Shripati recalls her devotion to Naranappa with enthusiasm, "in a hundred mile radius is there any woman as lovely, as bright, as good, as Chandri? . . . What does it matter if she's a whore? . . . Didn't she behave better than any wife with Naranappa. . . . Which brahmin woman would do so much? Stupid shaven widows!" (72)

Chandri also possesses an acute practical sharpness. Unable to leave Naranappa's body rotting in his house, she tries to arrange his cremation. When Sheshappa indicates his inability to meddle with a brahmin corpse, she seeks the help of a Muslim acquaintance. Without bothering for religious rituals, she carries the corpse to the cremation ground and burns it, as she feels that it was only a carcass, a "stinking, rotten carcass," neither Brahmin, nor Shudra (70). She is also unwilling to create any complexities in Praneshacharya's life, and leaves the agrahara clandestinely. Her self-image is "matrilineal and she displays strong affections for her mother.[7] She desires a child by Praneshacharya as he had looks and also virtue. She is "a natural in pleasure, unaccustomed to self-reproach." (68) She does not want to publicize what had brought a sense of "worthwhileness" to her. (68) Suppressing her desire to meet the Acharya again, she quietly moves away, taking her jewellery and saris with her.

The unembellished surrender to passion which Praneshacharya had acknowledged in the presence of Chandri, is experienced by him again when Putta introduces him to Padmavati, a half-caste Malera woman living alone in a grove. This encounter is fraught with sexual implication, and parallels the earlier one with Chandri in the forest. She is presented as another "prostitute figure who tempts the ascetic Brahmin, stirring in him fires of passion."[8] Praneshacharya is mesmerized and transfixed, "Elongated dark eyes. A black snake braid coming down her shoulder, over her breast. The girl swaying at the end of the bamboo pole. Knives—wings—beaks—feathers. In the forest dark, the offering of full breasts. . . . The bird is paralyzed by the stare of the black serpent. . . . He turned around. . . . A stirring of fire in his chest. His eyes looked on, fiery." (123)

Women of *Samskara* are non-agentic stereotypical and non-autonomous characters who have internalized and adjusted to the patriarchal mores. Gendered constraints are corroborated and buttressed by the rigidity of the caste system, which further circumscribes the practicability of self-hood. The novel evocatively suggests how the social practices encourage a blinkered vision among men, which makes them insensitive to the individuality of women. Traditional chauvinistic values incite men to relate to women either within the pre-defined social roles or to treat them merely as sex objects. It shall be pertinent to refer to Virginia Woolf's path-breaking essay, "Men and Women," in which she has raised certain questions which are relevant in different backgrounds even today, though often get treated as cliches. Woolf has remarked that literature is not only a soliloquy of the garrulous male, it also often represents what men desire in women, and not what women essentially are. Similarly, sensitive readers can and do imagine what is not there, as what is not there also has a presence, it also has a tendency to creep in clandestinely and take over somehow highlighting the significance of what is not said, what has been deliberately marginalized to cloud vision. *Samskara* bears a testimony to it.

NOTES

1. Simone de Beauvoir, *The Second Sex*, trans. H.M. Parshley (London: Vintage, 1997), p. 131.
2. Rachel Alsop, Annette Fitzsimons, Kathleen Lunnon, *Theorizing Gender* (New York: Blackwell, 2002), p. 68.
3. Nalini Natarajan, "Gender and Caste: Modernity in U.R. Anantha Murthy's *Samskara*," Baral, Rao and Rath, ed., *U.R. Anantha Murthy's Samskara: A Critical Reader* (New Delhi: Pencraft International, 2005), p. 154.
4. *Ibid.*, p. 175.
5. E.M. Forster, *Aspects of the Novel* (New Delhi: Atlantic, 2001), p. 69.
6. *Ibid.*, 67.
7. Nalini Natarajan, p. 160.
8. Rajagopal Parthasarthy, "*Samskara*: The Passing of the Brahmin Tradition," Barbara Stoler Miller, ed., *Masterpieces of Asian Literature in Comparative Perspective* (New York: ME Sharpe), p. 197.

Quest for Meaning: Praneshacharya and Naranappa

Samskara had evoked serious controversy right after its publication in Kannada in 1965. It was accused of attacking Brahminism, particularly by those critics who interpreted the novel as a realistic rendition of a social problem. When the novel was made into a film in 1970, when its English translation was serialized in the *Illustrated Weekly of India*, also when the English translation by the eminent poet-translator A.K. Ramanujan came out in 1976, such controversies were raked repeatedly.[1] V.S. Naipaul emphasized the obscurantism of the 'barbaric civilization' where readers accept the "premises of the novel that are so difficult for an outsider: caste, pollution, the idea of the Karma-given self, the anguish at the loss of caste identity."[2] Ramanujan, in his *Afterword*, viewed the novel as an allegory rich in realistic detail. With his criticism the arena shifted "from a Hindu village community to the body and spirit of the protagonist."[3] However, the novel itself does not present any categorical conclusions. The multi-layered presence of subtexts, coupled with the total absence of any authorial comment, transfers the responsibility of decoding the textual message to the reader in a significant way, forcing him to take an ethical decision.

Samskara presents before us a community of persons who are interlocked with each other through various complex relationships—caste, economy, gender, societal hierarchy, religious questions and taboos ferment a complex web of relationships, against the backdrop of which the story line has been sketched. Superficially the novel deals with the dilemma of performing the last rites of Naranappa, a rebellious Brahmin who could not be excommunicated from his community by the rest of the Brahmins; yet at another level it also judges the quality of an entire way of life through two major characters, Praneshacharya and Naranappa, who are presented as foil and counterfoil to each other. These characters are affected, albeit in non-identical manner, by the traditions of their milieu, help to define it, and are absolute ends in themselves. *Samskara* posits the almost invincible constrictions of society in Indian milieu at places, yet strangely also enjoins the centre of value in individual human person—herein the motif of a quest, of a wandering meandering journey for searching out the selfhood, becomes urgent.

Raymond Williams has remarked that whereas the characteristic experience of the nineteenth century was to find a place and make a settlement, the characteristic experience of the 20th century is that of asserting and preserving an individuality.[4] The main characters of *Samskara*—Praneshacharya and Naranappa—corroborate it in their own ways. Their response to life and its challenges is highly individualistic and reflects their sensitivity.

Praneshacharya is introduced to us as a learned ascetic. "Crest-Jewel of Vedic Learning," he is the unquestioned spiritual guru of the agrahara brahmins. Even Naranappa grudgingly accepts that he epitomizes the traditional brahminic virtues, "My only sorrow is that there's no brahminism really left to destroy in this place—except you." (23) His only desire is to attain salvation, and for it he is willing to undergo severe trials. In his eagerness to attain it, he jumps the traditional advice of the *Varnashrama* system. The Indian concept of the *Varnashrama* postulates the division of an individual's life into four stages, i.e., *dharma*, *artha*, *kama* and *moksha*. The first is the stage of value addition and learning the righteous path. The second stage expects one to possess material affluence. The third stage expects an individual to fulfill familial responsibilities. Only after having satisfactorily experienced the first three stages, an individual can attain *moksha* or salvation, with its promise of irrevocable bliss. Praneshacharya transgresses the sequential expectations of the *Varnasharma* system. He marries an invalid and deliberately deprives him not only of conjugal happiness, but also of familial pleasures. Having a family is an extremely important part of the householder stage because the other stages do not produce offspring. The begetting of offspring is needed to ensure the continuance of the rites.[5] Absence of a male child sometimes may result in a highly problematic situation as it does in *Samskara* after Naranappa's death. Praneshacharya cannot be ignorant of such customs as the novel graphically delineates his familiarity with the mores of brahminic tradition. Before taking his own meal, he places the fodder before Gowri, the cow, and worshipfully caresses its body. He touches his own eyes with the hand that had touched the holy animal in a gesture of respect (2). When Chandri comes to announce Naranappa's death, he knows that he would be polluted after talking to her, a lowcaste concubine, and will have to bathe again before his meal (2). In such well-documented context one cannot conceive the Acharya's ignorance of the *Varnashrama* system. He also painstakingly takes care of his invalid wife, Bhagirathi. It gives him pleasure to think that such action would bring his *nirvana* a bit closer. His relationship with his wife is not based on love or mutual understanding. Despite his compassionate attitude towards her, a clandestine hypocrisy can be read in his attitude towards her. Bhagirathi on the other hand has been portrayed as a sensitive and traditional woman. She is aware of the barren nature of their marriage. She tells the Acharya, "A house needs a child to make it home. You've had no joy in this marriage." (1) But the Acharya feels that by marrying an invalid he gets "ripe and ready" for the ultimate salvation (2). Despite it, he comes across as a person of integrity and compassion, virtues which are reflected in all his deeds. He does not excommunicate Naranappa. Searching his conscience for an explanation of such decision, he finds answer in the infinite compassion of his heart, "was it only his threat to become a Muslim and pollute the agrahara that had kept the Acharya from excommunicating him? No, there was also compassion. The infinite compassion in his heart." (47) Material wealth does not tempt him. He returns Chandri's gold to her stating that she still has a life to live (49).

This revered, scholarly Brahmin is flabbergasted when he encounters Chandri while coming out of the Maruti temple. He had led a celibate life and is suddenly dwarfed by his raging passions when Chandri falls at his feet:

> His bending hand felt her hot breath, her warm tears; his hair rose in a thrill of tenderness and he caressed her loosened hair. The Sanskrit formula of blessing got stuck in his throat. As his hand played on her hair, Chandri's intensity doubled. . . . The Acharya's hunger, so far unconscious, suddenly raged, and he cried out like a child. (63)

The captivating seductive enticement of woman has always lured the ascetic saints in Hindu mythology. *Samskara* is also replete with such references. Anantha Murthy repeatedly alludes to the folklores of *matsyagandha*, Sage Vishvamitra and the temptress Menaka, Shakuntala and Sage Vyasa. Such parallels in a way highlight the necessity of leading a balanced life, of enjoying all aspects of life. Sidetracking the sensual in one's personality does not allow one to burgeon fully; Praneshacharya also realizes it. He abdicates the moral right of choosing the right course of action for the agrahara brahmins, and decides to admit his involvement with Chandri before other Brahmins:

> Chandri, get up. Let's go. Tomorrow morning when the Brahmins gather, we'll say this happened. You tell them yourself. As for my authority to decide for the agrahara, I have . . . lost it. If I don't have the courage to speak tomorrow you must speak out. I'm ready to do the funeral rites myself. I've no authority to tell any other brahmin to do them, that's all. (68)

The episode of Praneshacharya and Chandri illustrates the truth of the assertion made by Claude Levi-Strauss in his article "Incest and Myth" that the "incest prohibition is the basis of human society, in a sense it is the society."[6] Society made it necessary to establish a systematic nature of each kinship terminology and its corresponding set of marriage rules. It also evolved a coercive character for such rules and any violation of it was looked down upon. Calculus of the caste intensified such notions within the Indian social milieu. Simultaneously, the connections with the Oedipus legend are also well established in the relationship between Praneshacharya and Chandri: "the very precautions taken to avoid incest in fact make it inevitable . . . a sensational turn of events arises from the fact that two characters, originally introduced as distinct, are identified with each other."[7]

Praneshacharya is attracted towards Chandri's pliable erotic magnetism. His union with Chandri is the turning point of the novel, as henceforth he will not have the protection of his caste traditions, and shall be forced to face the existentialist dilemma of forging his own values and meanings in a kaleidoscopically changed world. He cannot claim obedience to any pre-existing and determining convention and has to confront the angst of the responsibility of making a choice. Praneshacharya decides to search for a meaningful after-life and decides to undertake a journey, rather an aimless wandering, in the hope of finding a release or a working-out of tensions in this personal-social problem. The experience of isolation and self-exile is an important part of the contemporary structure of feeling, and often used effectively within the framework of a realist novel.[8] Praneshacharya too decides to venture out into an unpredictable world—its isolating atmosphere has its own logic and may help him to get a better grip on the meanings of his life. Like Conrad's *Heart of Darkness* and Virginia Woolf's *The Voyage Out*, *Samskara* is based on the thematic motif of a quest—external as well as internal—though, unlike them, it does not provide any clear-cut answers. In some ways, the answer succeeds in getting back to questions. The grotesque side of life which is revealed to Praneshacharya once he undertakes the journey into the unknown also functions as a symbol of his turbulence, restlessness and fuzziness of emotions. At another level, Praneshacharya's journey symbolizes his growing and going out into the world, of his facing life as it is. His perceptions at this stage have the distinctive combination of passivity and action, and offer a statement of the difficulty of integrating the deepest needs of self-expression and self-realization with the life one must lead as a social being. The journey motif also demonstrates the disturbing confusion of the self's own needs and impulses, and of the horror contained in the fundamental inarticulate condition of that part of the mind from which attraction and revulsion arise.

The agrahara is famous not only because of the scholarship of Praneshacharya, it is also known for another brahmin Naranappa, "The agrahara had become famous in all ten directions—because of its legends, and also because of Praneshacharya, the great ascetic, 'Crest-Jewel of Vedic Learning,' who had settled down there, and certainly because of that scoundrel Naranappa." (17) The whole plot revolves round the question of performing the death-rites of Naranappa, even though the world-view of *Samskara* is actualized in consonance with the sensibility of Praneshacharya, not narrated from distance or held at arm's length, but taken as it is lived. The question of Naranappa's death-rites is central to the development of the plot, as it raises several questions regarding the essence and relevance of brahminism, leading ultimately to a journey for self-discovery. The questions which the novel raises possess cross correspondence and cannot be answered in isolation.

As soon as the brahmins come to know about Naranappa's death, they gather to discuss the issue of conducting his last rites. "Not a human soul there felt a pang at Naranappa's death, not even women and children. Still in everyone's heart an obscure fear, an unclean anxiety. Alive, Naranappa was an enemy; dead, a preventer of meals; as a corpse, a problem, a nuisance." (3) The brahmin wives warn their husbands, "Don't be in a hurry. Wait till Praneshacharya gives you a decision. Don't agree too quickly to perform the rites. You may do the wrong thing. The guru will excommunicate you." (4) During the meeting, other brahmins raise the question of his brahminhood. Garuda says that "the casteless scoundrel" should have been excommunicated earlier (11). Their fear mingles with greed when Chandri offers her ornaments for bearing the cost of Naranappa's death rites, and they vie with each other in lurid accounts of his misdeeds (10): he had induced Garuda's son, a boy who had studied Vedic scriptures, to run away from home and join army; he had also encouraged Lakshmana's son-in-law—an orphan nursed and brought up by Lakshmana—to desert his wife; he had also dynamited the fish tank of the Ganesha temple along with his Muslim friends and killed the fish which were dedicated to the lord for generations; he had demanded that the temple doors should also be opened for the lowcaste people; he also used to take food cooked by his lowcaste concubine Chandri. Will such a person still be treated as a brahmin? The brahmins voice their concern during their dialogue with Shankaracharya, the priest of a neighbouring village Prijatapura, "is Naranappa, who drank liquor and ate meat, who threw the holy stone into the river, is he a brahmin or is he not? Tell me, which of us is willing to lose his brahminhood here? Yet it's not at all right, I agree, to keep a dead brahmin's body waiting, uncremated." (9) The debate now centres on who can be termed as a brahmin, and also, interestingly, on can one lose one's caste! At this stage *Samskara* ceases to be a social documentary, the characters are no longer aspects of the society, the society becomes an aspect of the characters to raise probing questions about the prevalent and contemporarily accepted societal landscape. That is why *Samskara* cannot be responded to as the static realistic novel of a hardened convention. It echoes the characteristic experience of the twentieth century by ending with the motif of the quest. It is pertinent here to quote in detail the argument presented by Raymond Williams in his article "Realism and the Contemporary Novel":

> the characteristic experience of our century is that of asserting and preserving an individuality (again like much eighteenth-century experience) as compared with the characteristic nineteenth century experience of finding a place and making a settlement. The ordinary Victorian novel ends with a man going away on his own, having extricated himself from a dominating situation, and found himself in so doing. . . . In a time of great change, this kind of extrication and discovery was a necessary and valuable movement; the recorded individual histories amount to a common history. And while old establishments linger, and new establishments of a dominating kind are continually instituted, the breakaway has continually to be made, the personal assertion given form and substance, even to the point where it threatens to become the whole content of our literature.[9]

Praneshacharya and Naranappa are both questers. Naranappa had all along wanted to forge a new identity for himself, partly as a hedonist and partly as a reformer. He wanted to shake the very foundations on which the brahmin community had based its ethos. His loathing of its corrupt ways is palpable. He tells Praneshacharya, "Your Garuda, he robs shaven widows, he plots evil with black magic men, and he is one of your brahmins, isn't he? . . . All right, let's see who wins, Acharya, you or me? Let's see how long all this Brahmin business will last." (21) Further he says, "All your Brahmin respectability, I'll roll it up and throw it all ways for a little bit of pleasure with one female." (21) He is self-reliant and advocates a direct participation in life. He believes in imparting equal treatment to all castes. He is almost irreverent in his criticism of the upper caste practices of distancing themselves from others, "Your texts and rites don't work any more. The Congress Party is coming to power, you'll have to open up the temples to all outcastes." (21) He is the only character in the novel who, against the politically turbulent background of 1930s, shows any awareness of contemporary socio-political issues. Rest of the Brahmins, including Praneshacharya, are oblivious of the possibility of any changes in their familiar world. Several people are drawn towards him as he postulates new ideas and supports their realization. He is also a helpful person and possesses sharp business acumen. He had loaned money to Ahmad Bari, the fish merchant, to buy oxen when he was bankrupt (70). He had donated a harmonium to the Parijata Drama Group and was its prime mover (70). He also defies the brahminical taboos about partaking of food prepared by lower caste people. He eats food prepared by Chandri despite her hesitation (45). Chandri terms him as an "angry, mad, strong-willed man" who had never bowed to the social pressures. Within the precincts of a Brahmin agrahara, he openly lives with a lowborn concubine and threatens to turn Muslim if the brahmins excommunicate him. (45) He never repents about his actions and attitudes, though there is a hint that just before his death, his confidence had slightly wavered. Chandri recalls:

> But something gnawed at her now. It was weird. Naranappa, who wouldn't fold his hand before a god any time, had started talking strangely as his fever rose to his brain. As coma set in, he mum-

> bled, 'O mother! O God Ramachandra, Narayan!' cried out, 'Rama Rama.' Holy names. Not words that come out of a sinner's or an outcaste's mouth. She hadn't quite understood what was going on deep inside him (45)

Chandri's confusion about Naranappa's last words is not resolved. The novel does not provide any other reference for the interpretation of such hints. Is it a reflection of a sub-conscious desire to conform, a habitual action, or repentance? In the absence of any textual clues or interconnections nothing can be definitely said about it. On the basis of the internal evidence of the text, he comes across as a character who assertively can follow his own preferences.

Praneshacharya and Naranappa, both are intriguing characters. Instead of making simple choices in favour of life's dreary routine, they accept challenges. Again, the rejection of the existing reality is not merely subjective. Their choice is not merely a decorative function, it becomes a moral protest against the prevalent atmosphere which fails to satisfy their emotional and intellectual needs.

NOTES

1. Meenakshi Mukherjee, "*Samskara*," *U.R. Anantha Murthy's "Samskara": A Critical Reader*, Kailash C. Baral et al, ed. (New Delhi: Pencraft, 2005), p. 82.
2. Qtd. Meenakshi Mukherjee.
3. A.K. Ramanujan, *Afterword* to U.R. Anantha Murthy's *Samskara: A Rite for a Dead Man* (New Delhi: Oxford University Press), p. 141.
4. Raymond Williams, "Realism and the Contemporary Novel," David Lodge, ed., *20th Century Literary Criticism* (London: Longman, 1972), p. 589..
5. Christial Fornadel, http://www.haverford.edu./relg/sells/courses/rel101/P-vsystemin Samskara.com.
6. Claude Levi-Strauss, "Incest and Myth," David Lodge, p. 546.
7. *Ibid*, p. 548.
8. Raymond Williams, p. 586.
9. *Ibid.*, p. 589.

Irony, Satire and Humour in U.R. Anantha Murthy's *Samskara: A Rite for a Dead Man*

RAMESH K. SRIVASTAVA
Jhansi

U.R. Anantha Murthy's *Samskara* is a serious novel, dealing with the traditional ritual of the cremation of the dead body of a Brahmin. In the entire novel, Anantha Murthy has made an attempt to differentiate between the appearance and reality by adopting a series of literary devices, such as symbols, myths, irony, satire and humour, among others. The basic purpose behind Anantha Murthy's novel is his desire to show that a highly learned Brahmin, such as Praneshacharya, fails in understanding the reality of the world by adhering to the theoretical, bookish, outdated and even decadent traditions and rituals which have been responsible for the degeneration not only of Brahminism but also of Hinduism.

The novel *Samskara* opens with the dead body of Naranappa lying for cremation or *Samskara*. Though a Brahmin, Naranappa had lived the life of a pleasure-seeker, and if at all he had continued to be a Brahmin technically, it was because he was not expelled from Brahminism or evicted from an orthodox colony called agrahara. He drank liquor, ate meat and fish, abandoned his Brahmin wife and lived with a lowcaste woman named Chandri. Even though Naranappa's orthodox Brahmin friends had become very angry over his ways of living, they could not dare to throw him out of the Brahmin caste because of their own weaknesses, which he had exploited to his advantage.

Even though the novel is serious in tone, one can find some flashes of fun and humour, employed through imagery, hyperbole and caricature. Anantha Murthy has lampooned and blown to pieces the myths surrounding the orthodox and hypocritical

Brahmins by his use of powerful barbs soaked in honeyed comic vein, irony and satire. Such a strategy was essential keeping in mind the fact that the Brahmins occupied traditionally a preeminently high place and any direct criticism of their ways of living could have been quite explosive. The purpose of Anantha Murthy is to make the Brahmin community come out of their hypocritical holiness and to live a normal life. This could be done not by taking the bulls by their horns but to make them realize through irony, satire, humour as well as through myths and symbols so that the statements may appear to be good on surface but are quite devastating implicitly. That is also the reason that Anantha Murthy employs a low-keyed, tongue-in-cheek type of irony, satire and humour so that the orthodox Brahmin community does not take an immediate offence at the novel. There are reports that after the publication of this novel, there were wide-ranging protests against the portrayal of the degenerated Brahmins. It means that the novel did hurt them even when the attack was veiled. Anantha Murthy was thus successful in exposing the hypocrisy and vices of the Brahmins. Here is the description of the death of Naranappa—and the reactions of the Brahmins:

> The news of death spread like a fire to the other ten houses of the agrahara. Doors and windows were shut, with children inside. By god's grace, no Brahmin had yet eaten. Not a human soul there felt a pang at Naranappa's death, not even women and children. Still in everyone's heart an obscure fear, an unclean anxiety. Alive, Naranappa was an enemy; dead, a preventer of meals; as a corpse: a problem, a nuisance. (3)

The novelist writes about the heartlessness of the Brahmins—men and women—who did not feel any pain in the death of Naranappa. Instead, what worried them was an unknown fear that Naranappa might create a problem, even in his death and, consequently, all the Brahmins, including women and children, may not be able to have their regular meals. It is a matter of pity that the Brahmins should fall so low in their selfishness as to worry about their meals while the dead body, lying for cremation, requires their urgent attention. Anantha Murthy writes of many sins that the Brahmins of agrahara committed, including those of gluttony, of avarice and love of gold. What covered them all was the "terrific virtue" of Praneshacharya but that only encouraged them to commit more sins. They show their greed for gold on the occasion of cremation of Naranappa's body. Initially opposed to it, some of them change their views the moment Chandri, the mistress of Naranappa, comes to Praneshacharya, requesting him for a decent cremation of Naranappa, and offers her gold ornaments for it. Durgabhatta eyes Chandri greedily, thinking of her as a "precious object," having sharpness in her features as described in Vatsyayana's book of love. He looked at her breasts and thought

> In sex, she's the type who sucks the male dry. Her eyes, which should be fickle, are now misty with grief and fear, but she looks good that way. Like Matsyagandhi, the Fisherwoman in the Ravi Verma print hung up in Durgabhatta's bedroom, shyly trying to hide her breasts bursting through her poor rag of a sari. The same eyes and nose: no wonder Naranappa threw away the worship-stone for her, ate taboo meat and drank taboo liquor. (8)

The death of Naranappa should have made Durgabhatta sober, melancholic, philosophical and introspective; instead, it arouses his dormant passions towards the mistress of Naranappa. If Durgabhatta had an opportunity, he too would have abandoned his Brahminism for a pretty woman like Chandri the same way as Naranappa had. Hence his concern for the degeneration of Brahminism is merely an eyewash. If Praneshacharya were not present and if the dead body of Naranappa had not been lying there, Durgabhatta might have quoted some lines from romantic poetry to the Brahmins present there whose life he had found quite uninteresting and barren. A young Brahmin Shripati, after taking some liquor, sings of the beauty of Chandri, saying, "Whatever anybody may say. Whatever Brahmins bray—I swear—what do you say?—in a hundred-mile radius is there any woman as lovely, as bright, as good, as Chandri? Take a count. If you find one, I'll give up my caste." (72) Other Brahmins like Manjunatha also take drinks though aware of the fact that the dead body of Naranappa lies uncremated there. After taking the second bottle of liquor, Shripati says, "Our best friend is lying there dead, rotting! No one to take care of his rites. And what are we doing here, having a good time?" (73)

Anantha Murthy exaggerates some traits, some habits and even some weaknesses of Garudacharya, but through him, he is broadly hinting at the problems of most of Brahmins. Garuda and Lakshmana had been related to Naranappa. Praneshacharya recollects the words of Naranappa who had forewarned him, even challenged him, about the degeneration of Brahmins, and had particularly made fun of Brahminism of Garuda, among others.

> Let's see who wins in the end—you or me. I'll destroy brahminism. I certainly will. My only sorrow is that there's no brahminism really left to destroy in this place—except you. Garuda, Lakshmana, Durgabhatta—ahaha—what brahmins! If I were still a Brahmin, that fellow Garudacharya would have washed me down with his *aposhana* water. Or that Lakshmana—he loves money so much he'll lick a copper coin off a heap of shit. He will tie another wilted sister-in-law round my neck, just to get at my property. And I'd have had to cut my hair to a tuft, smear charcoal on my face, sit on your verandah and listen to your holy-holy yarns. (23)

In the above passage the words of Naranappa may appear to be highly exaggerated, particularly his claim that he would destroy Brahminism or that there is no Brahminism left out to be destroyed, what he had bluntly uttered was truth. How fragile, how brittle Brahminism appears which cracks under the threat of one person—Naranappa—who had done everything *openly* contrary to what is permissible in agrahara, but most Brahmins were too weak to do anything against him. If they had taken action against him, he had threatened: "Try and excommunicate me now. I'll become a Muslim, I'll get you all tied to pillars and cram cow's flesh into your mouths and see to it personally that your sacred brahminism is ground into the mud." (11)

The decadence of brahminism becomes unambiguously clear by the end of the novel. When Naranappa says that Lakshmana is so greedy that "he'll even lick a copper coin off a heap of shit," (24) he portrays the real weakness of Brahmins for money. Through Naranappa, Murthy demolishes the myths surrounding

Brahmins by attacking not only their greed for money and gold but also for the marriages which are arranged not so much according to the ruling stars, or on the bases of *gunas* in the horoscopes but for economic gains. Anantha Murthy shows that it is not so much Naranappa who is degenerated as the rest of the Brahmin community in agrahara is. Most of the Brahmins portrayed in the novel are hypocritically selfish, greedy, narrow-minded and even short-sighted, but who take shelter behind the ancient Hindu classics, their high-sounding principles and the traditional morality which serve as masks to hide their ugly self. In contrast, Naranappa may appear to be unbrahminical by taking liquor, eating meat and living with Chandri, but he is at least true to himself.

Throughout the novel, the underlying concern of the Brahmins is not for the cremation of Naranappa's dead body but when would they be able to take meals! This is what they perpetually ask Praneshacharya about. How long would they be required to remain hungry? Garudacharya tells Praneshacharya:

> Haven't you yourself said, there's such a thing as a dharma, a rule for emergencies? Didn't you—what—once suggest that if a man's life depended on it we could feed him even cow's flesh—such a thing wouldn't be a sin—didn't you say? What do you say—a story you told us once—sage Vishvamitra, when the earth was famine-stricken, found hunger unbearable, and ate dog-meat, because the supreme dharma is the saving of a life?—What do you say? (30)

Garudacharya's request to Praneshacharya is obviously to treat the cremation of Naranappa's dead body as an emergency so that the lives of many hungry Brahmins could be saved by letting them take meals with or without the cremation of Naranappa's dead body. Not finding any solution coming from Praneshacharya which could satisfy their hunger, Dasacharya suggested that they could go to Kaimara agrahara and eat there: "We'll walk to Kaimara and change our polluted sacred threads. Won't the Brahmins there offer us a meal? You shouldn't eat in the agrahara where a dead body lies uncremated, but is there any objection to eating in Kaimara? What do you say?" (79) Consequently, the Brahmins leave the agrahara so that they could avoid being starved. Durgabhatta got his bullock-cart ready and took his wife and children to his mother-in-law's place. Lakshmanacharya remembered to take some banana leaves and leaf-cups which he was asked for earlier. Dasacharya took some puffed rice for the road, and decided to go to Lakshmana's in-laws. Praneshacharya too could have gone with these Brahmins to Kaimara but his wife began to have her menstruation period. When they had taken baths at Kaimara, Subhannacharya offered them meals. The Brahmins were anxiously waiting for this invitation and "poured down hot steaming rice and *saru* into their bellies till it touched the Supreme Spirit inside." (80)

Among the entire crowd of Brahmins living in agrahara, there was one person—Praneshacharya—who shone as a bright star, setting an example before others. A great learned Brahmin, he had defeated a number of other learned Brahmins in discussion. Taken as a model Brahmin, he had devoted his life for the preservation of Brahminical traditions. Others looked upon him as a guide to show the path on the complex question of what is to be done to the dead body of Naranappa who was a Brahmin by birth but who had violated all the norms of Brahminical life. Praneshacharya reads out the text of the religious books in order to find a solution to the vexed problem of Naranappa's cremation, but in vain. He goes to the temple to seek God's help in the matter but he too, succumbs to Chandri's temptation and has sex with her. Anantha Murthy refers to Praneshacharya's "body's tigerish lust" which was "tamed by a righteousness" but "at the touch of Chandri's breast, the animal leaped to its natural self and bared its teeth." (81) By making use of a brilliant stroke of irony and satire, Anantha Murthy raises Praneshacharya to the pinnacle of height, sets him as a model, an ideal—someone to be emulated—and then removes the base from under his feet, making him fall headlong so that he becomes no different—or even worse—than other hypocritical Brahmins! However, the saving grace is that he himself realizes his weaknesses, and thus it becomes pardonable: "Like a baby monkey losing hold of his grip on the mother's body as she leaps from branch to branch, he felt he had lost hold and fallen from the rites and actions he had clutched till now." (75)

Anantha Murthy has used the device of parallel and contrast by ironically placing side by side two kinds of deaths—that of the Brahmins and the rats. After the death of Naranappa, the Brahmins show their overriding interest in taking meals, as if dying of hunger. With the outbreak of plague in Shivamogge, the rats move in a circular motion on their tails and fall down dead. On the other hand, Brahmins go into circles over the question of taking meals while Naranappa's dead body lies uncremated. Some of them take meals stealthily and a couple of them die in the process. Thus the most eminently placed Brahmins in the hierarchy of Hindu caste system are brought down and compared ironically with the hungry and dying rats. In their deaths, the Brahmins lie as uncared for as are the rats. The dead body of Naranappa instead of having a proper cremation was burnt by Chandri and a Muslim cart man. Some Brahmins die on way to Kaimara and are left unattended the same way as the dead rats also lie unattended. As a matter of fact, the rats are better placed than the Brahmins because at least the eagles are waiting for the final disposal of dead bodies of rats, but probably the Brahmins like Naranappa are not that lucky. On another level, Anantha Murthy also compares Brahmins with eagles. After the death of Naranappa, Brahmins have been portrayed as hungry as eagles; the former wait for food while the latter for dead rats. Whereas eagles and crows are scavenging birds fated to cleaning the rotting dead bodies and are therefore indulging in their legitimate action of cleaning the dead bodies of rats, Brahmins are expected to perform the last rites of other human beings, particularly of the Brahmins, with the chants of holy mantras according to Vedic rites. The scavenging birds—*sudras* in human terms—do their duties, but the Brahmins fail. In the hierarchy of duty performers, Anantha Murthy has placed Brahmins at the lowest level—lower than the *sudras*. When Anantha Murthy compares idealized human beings with low, scavenging birds, he shows symbolically that the degenerated Brahmins are worse than the *sudras* or untouchables of the sweeping class.

There is also a glaring contrast between the Brahmins and non-Brahmins. When viewed in totality, the Brahmins come out worse off than the non-Brahmins, and lower also to the degenerated Brahmins. Take the cases of Naranappa and his mistress Chandri. Naranappa abandoned his Brahmin wife and was keeping a lowcaste woman Chandri as his mistress. He does everything contrary to Brahminical norms, and is therefore considered a degenerated Brahmin. However, Anantha Murthy places him way above the so-called pure Brahmins who have been portrayed as greedy, myopic, selfish and hypocrite. A true picture is portrayed by the 70-year old Lakshmidevamma who stands before Garudacharya's house, calling him a "ruiner of towns" and a "widow-taker." Between Garudacharya and Naranappa, she considers the former the more dangerous of the two:

> You villain! A golden man like Naranappa became an outcaste, got himself a harlot. You fellows call yourself Brahmins, you sit there and don't want to take out a dead man's body. Where has your brahminism gone, you rascals! . . . Brahminism is in ruins. Why don't you shave your heads and become Muslims, why do you need to be Brahmins, you! (43)

Shripati contrasts Brahmin women with a non-Brahmin Chandri, showering praises not only of Chandri's beauty but also of her virtues as a faithful woman.

> What does it matter if she's a whore? You tell me, didn't she behave better than any wife with Naranappa? If he drank too much and vomited, she wiped up the mess. She even wiped ours up, didn't she? Anytime, even at midnight, when he woke her up she cooked and served him, all smiles. Which Brahmin woman would do so much? Stupid shaven widows! (72)

Praneshacharya is contrasted with Putta. When Praneshacharya ran away from agrahara, it was Putta with whom he covered some distance. Interestingly, Putta is not a Brahmin but Anantha Murthy has portrayed him, in some respects better than Praneshacharya. The novelist describes the two thus:

> Putta of the Maleras stuck to Praneshacharya like a sin of the past. That was his way; if you stop, he will stop too; sit, he'll sit. Walk

> faster, he'll walk faster; if slower, slower. Won't leave your side. Praneshacharya was getting quite upset. He'd like to be alone, sit with his eyes shut, and think for himself—but this fellow Putta is rattling away ceaselessly. (106)

Though Putta's portrait has been drawn in somewhat comic terms, more so when he assumes many personalities. He becomes a riddle man, giving Praneshacharya one riddle and then other. When Praneshacharya purposefully became a dull-witted person, Putta laughed loudly and immediately solved the puzzle. It is ironical how Putta pities Praneshacharya, considers him good, but not a very clever Brahmin. Putta talks about his wife, calling her "a fusspot" and both Praneshacharya and Putta laugh. He is called Riddleman Putta and Prattling Putta or Putta, the Altruist. His activities are child-like. At the festival in Melige, he enjoyed the song of the balloon-seller, the Bombay Box showing pictures through a hole, and an acrobat show, but Praneshacharya could not come down to enjoy the world of ordinary pleasures. "In all this bustle and busyness, amid noises of balloons and pipes, the soda-pop and the sweetmeats, the peal of temple bells, the gorgeous spectacle of women's bangle shops, Praneshacharya walked as one entranced, following Putta" (115). Then they saw a cock-fight and Praneshacharya felt as though he had visited "a demoniac world." A.K. Ramanujan calls Putta "Praneshacharya's initiator into the mysteries of the ordinary and the familiar, the purity of the regenerate, the wholeness of the crude" (*Afterword*, 142)

Putta is complementary to Praneshacharya, the former representing the missing self of the latter. He is the projection of Praneshacharya's unfulfilled cravings—an indirect wish-fulfillment. Given a choice, Praneshacharya would have liked to lead the kind of life that Putta does. Anantha Murthy suggests that Praneshacharya is merely a theoretical Brahmin who has studied the religious classics well but is ignorant of the life in the world around him. Putta has seen a great deal of life, but has not read any religious classics and therefore he, too, is incomplete in himself. One lacks life; the other lacks learning. They are two sides of the same coin. Neither of them is complete in himself but is complementary to the other. Despite good knowledge of Hindu rites and rituals, Praneshacharya fails to do anything in the right way, whereas Putta with his common sense keeps the former happy without losing touch with the realistic world.

Where are wit and humour and what is their function in portraying the hypocritical lives of Brahmins? The incident of the death of Naranappa, and the lack of concern of the hypocritical and greedy Brahmins are quite painful which make the reader unhappy by bringing to his mind the grim picture of traditionally highly-placed Brahmins who in reality are so degenerated and decadent that they bring to the reader a sense of disillusionment and disgust. But this is also precisely the place where the reader chuckles by noticing that the highest are not really the highest, and that these Brahmins have the same weaknesses and vices which the readers are believed to have. It is here that an invisible bond, even if tenuous and fragile, is established between the reader and Naranappa who was despised by the rest of Brahmin community of agrahara. The illustrious, shining and glowing lives of the great Brahmins which had awed the reader for centuries, had made him feel inferior to them, now get a sense of relief, even pleasure on the revelation that all that glitters is not gold and the pious souls are not really that pious. The contrasting picture creates a vast chasm into the worlds of appearance and of reality, and the reader feels somewhat amused by it.

Even though Anantha Murthy's powerful instruments of attack are irony and satire, some of the images are fresh, witty, funny, odd or exaggerated, and give delight to the reader. A.K. Ramanujan writes: "the book's allegoric and narrative power marshals enough poetic images, ideas, stereotypes, and caricatures." (*Afterword*, 145) A hungry Dasacharya—a poor Brahmin—is thin and bony as a sick cow. He "lived entirely on the meals that Brahmins get at death-rites and anniversaries. He would walk ten miles for such a meal any day." (8) Now his worry is that if Naranappa were cremated properly, even when he had violated Brahminical rules, all the Brahmins of agrahara would be ill-known and, therefore, not invited for a brahmin meal. Dasacharya "fondled his belly as a mother fondles a crying child" (34) and thought he would die if he missed his meals. "Hunger beat drums in their bellies and banished sleep, giving red eyes to the Brahmins" (51). When Chandri places her gold ornaments before Praneshacharya, "the eyes of the poorer Brahmins like Dasa grew moist, their mouths watered." (10) Lakshmanacharya, nagged by his wife to claim Chandri's gold, reached Praneshacharya's house but to Garuda, he appeared "suddenly like a bear let loose in the middle of a service for Shiva." (33) Garudacharya in his anger is compared to Durvasa, who "jumped about as if overrun by red ants, shouting." (27) When Sitadevi wanted Garudacharya to claim gold ornaments so that they could buy off their son from the military bond, Garuda "stepped like a thief" (28) into Praneshacharya's house. Belli, while making love with Shripati "twists like a snake" and after taking her father's toddy becomes "warm and ready—like a tuned-up drum." (37) In her readiness to make love with Shripati, she "had always been like ripe ears of corn bending before the falling rain." (40) Rats come out "like a wedding procession." (58) An eagle sat on a brahmin house "unafraid, defiant, like a shameless kinsman." (59) The vulture on their roof "curved his neck around like a danseuse." (59) The agrahara street is "so hot you could pop corn on it." (17) Though all these images may not be funny and humorous, most of them are odd, hyperbolic, and cause one to chuckle.

In addition to these short images, Anantha Murthy gives a series of flitting images as if in a cinematic motion. These images lighten the tension which the uncremated body of Naranappa has generated. Here are the images of the fair:

> A crowd milled around the temple chariot. Another crowd around the sodawater shop. Still another, around the man with the performing monkey. Children's toy trumpets, balloons. In the midst of these noises, a demon, an evil spirit. A town-crier. Beating his tom tom, he announced in his loud town-crier voice: "There's a plague in Shivamogge! The epidemic of Mari! Any one going to Shivamogge should stop at Tirthahalli and get an inoculation! That's the order of the Municipality!" People listened to him with interest, and drank more sodawater. Laughed in guffaws at the antics of the

> monkey. A bilingual expert spoke in Urdu and Kannada, selling his medicine to the gathered crowd: "Just one anna, one anna, *ek ana, ek ana*. For stomach-aches, ear-aches, diabetes, arthritis, children's diseases, menstrual troubles, itches and typhoid—take this pill. Pundits from Kerala have prepared this pill with magic chants. Just one anna *ek ana, ek ana*. . . ." The Bombay Box man was dancing: "Look, look at the Tirupati God. Timmappa! Look, look at the courtesan of Bombay!" An acrobat slid in a flash down the slope of a rope tied between a branch above and a peg on the floor, and came to his feet with a salute. A man suddenly slapped a little boy for wanting a balloon. The boy cried loudly. A gramophone song from the coffee shop. Sweetmeats of many colours in the Muslim shop. The drawling intonation of the peasants and their women. (126)

The flitting images of various scenes of the fair given above show that a general atmosphere of indifference to the problems of others characterizes not only the Brahmins but most human beings irrespective of their age, caste, or community. This indifference extends even to their own beings when both peasants and urban people do not take precaution even after the announcement by the town-crier that the plague has broken out in Shivamogge and they must get themselves inoculated at Tirthahalli. The serious order of the Municipality concerning their own health is laughed away in loud guffaws. An acrobat, a pill-selling expert and the antics of the monkeys interest these people more but not the dying rats, the breaking out of the plague, nor even the dead body of Naranappa waiting for cremation. It is natural that certain Brahmin communities felt that "Brahmin men and women were unfairly caricatured" (*Afterword*, 146).

Even though Anantha Murthy presents in the novel some of the most serious issues concerning life, the underlying tone throughout the novel is somewhat light, as if he were a good physician trying to keep his serious patients in good humour. His use of caricature falls in the same category and serves two purposes. First of all, it distorts the picture of a person by highlighting some of his weak traits, and secondly, it provokes humour and fun for the readers even if at someone's cost. In the following paragraph, Anantha Murthy describes the hunger of Lakshmanacharya, as also his deshaped body:

> "True . . . true . . . quite true," said Lakshmanacharya, rubbing his belly—jerking his face forwards and backwards, batting his eyelids rapidly. The only well-fed part of his body was his belly, swollen with malarial bubo. Sunken cheeks, yellow eyes deep in sockets, ribs protruding, a leg twisted—altogether an unbalanced body. The rival brahmins of Parijatapura mocked at him for walking with his buttocks out. (4)

Here the concern of Lakshmanacharya obviously is his own hunger, not the cremation of Naranappa. The absence of a well-balanced body of Lakshmanacharya, particularly his swollen belly, becomes a symbol of the entire Brahmin community whose prime concern seems to be their own hunger and greed unmindful of what happens to the other members of the community. See what Garuda thinks of Lakshmanacharya:

> This fellow doesn't buy a spoon of oil for his bath, his fist is rigid as stone; this is the meanest of Brahmins. Who in the agrahara doesn't know it? When his wife nags him about an oil-bath he gets up in the morning and walks four miles to the Konkaniman's shop. "Hey, Kamat, have you any fresh sesame oil? Is it any good? What does it sell for? It isn't musty, is it? Let me see." With such patter he cups his hands and gets a couple of spoons as sample, pretends to smell it and says: "It's all right, still a bit impure. Tell me when you get real fresh stuff, we need a can of oil for our house." And smears the oil all over his head. Then he puts his hands into the sack of red peppers, and while asking the price, picks up a fistful and transfers it to his bag, all the while chatting casually. From there he walks a mile to Shenoy's shop; there he slanders Kamat's shop, and picks up another couple of spoons of oil for his bath and for a fresh-cooked meal. Then he forages again in someone or other's grove, brings home some cuts of banana-leaf to dry them in the sun and make leaf-cups which he will sell for a few pice. Or sells sacred thread to make a few more pice. Waits like a vulture to get invited to meals. Now his eyes are on the gold. Come what may—one must see to it that he doesn't get the loot. (34-35)

Lakshmidevamma, 70-year old widow, has been caricatured well. When unable to sleep, she would stand before Garudacharya's house, "invoke sons and grandsons and ancestors, summon gods and goddesses for witness, throw fistful of curses at him." She would then go to sleep after closing the door with loud noise. Anantha Murthy goes on further, "Her door and her belch were *famous* in the agrahara. Both could be heard from one end to the other. Her *fame* had spread to the Brahmin colonies in all four directions. Because she was a child-widow, they called her Lakshmidevamma the Ill-Omen. . . . They all called her Sour Belch. But her *best known name* was Half-Wit Lakshmidevamma." (42, my italics) Anantha Murthy uses words "famous," her "fame," and her "best known name" ironically whereas his intention is otherwise. Garudacharya has been ridiculed for his "nasal sentences punctuated by his what-do-you-says" but which get "spurred on again once he takes two more pinches of snuff." (5)

Praneshacharya, who in the first half of the novel is portrayed as a sober and idealistic Brahmin, becomes a butt of Anantha Murthy's criticism in the latter part. He is caricatured well when he tries to escape his own identity. When Praneshacharya was recognized at the temple where he was taking his meals, he ran away. Putta describes his action in the following words: "What's this Swami? Not a word, and you're running like someone in a hurry to go to the bathroom for a big job" (133). Putta laughed but went on to justify the Acharya's action, "These things do happen. Calls of nature became most urgent right in the middle of dinner. I thought that is what happened to you, so I felt like laughing." (134)

Irony and humour come out more clearly in the second or successive readings of Anantha Murthy's *Samskara*. The reader knows that towards the end of the novel, Praneshacharya had sex with Chandri, wanted to live with her, and was not averse to sleeping with Padmavati who was a half-caste Malera. He even thought amorously of Belli who had sex with Shripati. But as one goes over to the beginning of the novel, Praneshacharya believes that if he talked to Chandri, "he would be polluted; he would have to bathe again before his meal." (2) He had studied in Kashi, knew all the scriptures—and had earned the title

"Crest-Jewel of Vedic Learning." But as one reads the novel, it becomes clearer than ever, that a non-Brahmin Chandri is much greater than all the Brahmins put together. Though born to a family of prostitutes, and hence supposed to be faithful to none, Chandri is more faithful to Naranappa than other Brahmins are to their wives—Garudacharya, Durgabhatta, Shripati, Praneshacharya, and so on. She offers her gold ornaments for the expenses of the rites of Naranappa. She cannot take rest until his dead body is properly cremated. Anantha Murthy showers some choicest eulogical expressions on Chandri, comparing her with the Tunga river:

> Born to a family of prostitutes, she was an exception to all rules. She was ever-auspicious, daily-wedded, the one without widowhood. How can sin define a running river? It's good for a drink when a man's thirsty, it's good for a wash when a man's filthy, and it's good for bathing the god's images with; it says Yes to everything, never a No. Like her, doesn't dry up, doesn't tire. Tunga, river that doesn't dry, doesn't tire. (44)

After ensuring a proper cremation of Naranappa's body, Chandri wanted to go away to Kundapura and "weep for him there." She had eaten his salt and must remain true to him. This is precisely what she does. Ironically, Praneshacharya who in the beginning of the novel did not want to talk to Chandri for fear of being polluted, towards the end pales before her in goodness, fidelity and in fulfilling moral obligations.

Since the novel is about the cremation of a dead body, not many children have been introduced in the novel. However, in one scene of the novel, Venkataramanacharya's naughty children and their naturally funny activities bring a little humour in the novel even if it is not very pleasant. The children stood in the backyard counting the dying rats falling down from the storerooms into the yard. They clapped their hands and counted the dead rats in the same way as their parents must have often counted measures of paddy:

> gain-O gain
> two-O two

> three-O three
> four-O four
> five-O five
> six-O six
> one more-O one-more (51)

Their mother's reprimand did not diminish the children's enthusiasm and glee in shrieking, clapping, leaping and yet continuing their counting activities: "Look Ma, look eight-O eight, . . . Ten rats! Look Ma, look!" (52) When they were herded together in a room, they saw the appearance of a rat which turned round and round, and made the children mightily delighted, because their ignorance and innocence insulate them from the perception of grim situation and the impending catastrophe.

The use of English in India has often been a good source of humour. The ignorance of its grammatical rules, its confusing pronunciation, its regional variations, and the literal translations from vernacular sentences have often provided a lot of humour and fun in many Indian English novels, e.g. in Mulk Raj Anand, Bhabani Bhattacharya, Khushwant Singh and Arundhati Roy. In *Samskara*, Shripati criticizes the hypocritical Brahmins. Manjunatha agreed with Shripati but in his ignorance of English uttered only "Yus, yus," because this was one of the three words of English he knew and over which Nagaraja laughed, saying, "If you give Manjunatha a drink, he'll speak English." (73)

Drunkenness also becomes a minor source of humour. Shripati, Manjunatha and Nagaraja had drinks after which they decided to cremate their friend Naranappa's dead body. Here is an account of how they all behave:

> The liquor had gone straight to their heads; they went into the agrahara, to Naranappa's door, gave it a push, and went in fearlessly. The liquor had made them insensitive to the stench. They went upstairs. Shripati beamed his flash light all around. Where? Where? Naranappa's corpse was nowhere. All five of them suddenly feared for their lives. Nagaraja said, "Ha, Naranappa has become a spirit, and has walked away." As soon as he said that, they dropped the bag of liquor bottles and all five ran for their lives.

> When Half-Wit Lakshmidevamma, sleepless, opened her thunderous door and came out into the agrahara street to curse everybody, she saw them. She shrieked, "Look, look at the demons! And let out a long belch: *Hee. . . .* eey!" (73-74)

Sometimes humour and pathos go together in the novel. The condition of hungry Dasacharya, which was a matter of mockery and fun, becomes pathetic once he fears he would die if he did not eat rightaway. Anantha Murthy describes his pathetic plight: "The smells of all that food cooking for the children, O to smell them on this fasting day! It was like melted butter poured into a burning fire. He spat out some of the rising spittle in his mouth, and swallowed some of it." (55) When Manjayya invites Dasacharya to eat some *uppittu*, the latter inwardly wants to eat but pathetically cries, "But if those rascals in our agrahara hear about it, no one will invite me to a ceremony again. What can I do, Manjayya?" (56) And as Manjayya assures him that he would not tell anyone about it, and the moment the word *uppittu* is uttered, "the bowels in Dasacharya's belly turned and made loud gurgling noises." (57) Since the cooked rice could not have been eaten in a Smarta house, Dasacharya had milk, jaggery, flat rice, plantains and honey. He was persuaded to have some *uppittu* also after which he "rubbed his belly to the rhythm of the name of the Supreme Spirit, and didn't say No." (57)

U.R. Anantha Murthy's *Samskara* is a powerful indictment of orthodox and hypocritical Brahmins, well-soaked in irony and satire, but made somewhat palatable with occasional sprinkling of fun and humour. While the reading of the novel is like journeying through a dark tunnel on a pitch dark night, a brief even if rare cessation of grimness, the inclusion of a light-hearted remark, an odd image, or a teasing peculiarity come like the flashing light of a glowworm, or like the brief wavering light of a matchstick which may not be adequate to guide a doomed and dispirited traveller but becomes good enough to momentarily revitalize his drooping spirits and make him move forward. The novel is a powerful medicament with flavouring agents for the alleviation of cancerous ills of a section of the Hindu society.

Chandri: A Lowcaste Harlot or a *Samskari* Woman?

TEJINDER KAUR
Punjabi University, Patiala

The task of deciding the topic for writing a paper for the present anthology on Anantha Murthy's *Samskara* (1978) subtitled *A Rite for a Dead Man* was an arduous one as the reading and re-readings of the text leave you with so many questions without giving conclusive answers. There is a continuous deferment of the questions and their suggestive answers, producing new meanings during and after every reading which make this text a "writerly" one (Roland Barthes's term). The title and the sub-title of the text rightly give us the impression of its being a narrative pertaining to the *Samskara*, the last rite of a dead man. The central focus of the fabula is the dead body of a heretic, Naranappa—belonging to Madhva brahmin caste—lying waiting in the agrahara—a brahmin colony—of a Karnataka village named Durvasapura to be cremated (since he was an orphan and also had no children to perform his last rites) putting the brahmins of that agrahara into religious controversy as to who should do this task without losing his brahminhood and should his *Samskara* be performed as per the prescribed norms for his high caste in the holy texts as he had been following the anti-brahminic ways. The syuzhet of the narrative is woven by the writer around this problematic to dwell and debate on so many issues in multiple voices which keep on mounting and conflicting as the action moves and even after the narrative ends in the text. In this polyphonic novel, to borrow Bakhtin's words, "everything is still in the future and will always be in the future." (1984: 166)

Another problematic of this text is the multiple meanings of the Sanskrit word 'Samskara' "which refers to concept central to Hinduism" quoted by the translator A.K. Ramanujan from a Kannada English Dictionary by the Reverend F. Kittel, Mangalore, 1894, p.1479. Among its various meanings are forming well, refining, refinement, making sacred, making pure, purification, purity, a sanctifying or purificatory rite or essential ceremony (enjoined on all the first three classes or castes), any rite or ceremony, funeral obsequies (Epigraph, *Samskara*) which prompt us to explicate the text and analyze the intentions and conduct of its characters from various angles. Though the word 'Samskara' does not occur obtrusively or too frequently in the narrative, its meanings implicitly inform the action. . . .the action depends on the several meanings being at loggerheads with each other." (Afterword, *Samskara*) In Derrida's words, we can say, "The absence of the transcendental signified extends the domain and the play of signification infinitely." (110)

The focal point of the novel is no doubt the problem-generating corpse of Naranappa who in his lifetime had openly flouted, mocked at and questioned the prescribed ideology and code of conduct for his caste, and exposed the hypocritical and sinful living of the fellow Brahmins, giving a challenge to the most virtuous brahmin there Praneshacharya "the Crest-jewel of Vedic learning," the local Guru and of the nearby agraharas, by saying once, "All your brahmin respectability. I'll roll it up and throw it all ways for a little bit of pleasure with one female." (21) He had been living a life of his own desire without bothering about the good or bad opinions of his fellow agraharians by deserting his non-pleasure giving wife, living happily for the last ten years with a beautiful concubine (lowcaste) Chandri brought from Kundapura, eating food cooked by her, eating meat and catching fish from the temple pond with Muslims, having cut his tuft growing the crop of hair in the western style, forming drama and dance troupes and goading the brahmin youth of his own and nearby agraharas to give up the orthodox and redundant thinking and way of life. But this focus gets decentred with the actions and movements.of many characters as multiple voices grapple with multiple individual problems and questions in their own encounters with different situations and dilemmas.

There are apparently two male protagonists in the novel—Naranappa, the condemned one, and Praneshacharya, who is shown in constant conflict, agony and dilemma in the second half of the novel, struggling internally to find his own answers to many problems but if we analyze the causes of their predicament, it is their involvement with Chandri, a lowcaste harlot (considered to be un-*samskari*—impure, unrefined, uncultured because of her birth from a prostitute's womb) who was brought by Naranappa to this hamlet inhabited by the higher caste brahmins (supposed to be *samskari*—pure, refined, cultured since born in brahmin families)—men and women. Naranappa's open living with Chandri had caused commotion in the entire agrahara during his lifetime and now even after his death leaving the fellow brahmins hungry and angry. Though no one in the agrahara is shown to be aware of Praneshacharya's chance nocturnal sexual encounter with her but the latter half of the text deals with his acute sense of guilt, a series of self-introspections and self-analyses, dwindling between "asceticism and eroticism," "dḥarma and kama," between his desires aroused by the touch of Chandri's flesh and his mask of a renowned scholar and ascetic practitioner of brahminic way of life, and his final resolve to go to Kundapura, locate Chandri, start living with her fearlessly and "remake himself" after confessing his encounter with her before the brahmins of the agrahara who must have returned after visiting their Guru and seeking his guidelines regarding the last rites of Naranappa, and to cremate Naranappa's dead body himself as like Naranappa he himself had fallen from the sacred path. Much has been written about the various issues revolving around both these characters but a scanty attention has been drawn towards Chandri who though staying in the background is the cause of bringing them to the foreground. Moreover, it is her silent but good-intentioned actions which trigger the further moves in the novel and give them dramatic turns.

Caste, social status and profession wise Chandri is a whore, an outcaste and is dubbed as "Mari" (the dark goddess of death, plague etc.) by Garudacharya, "a seducing witch," "a filthy whore" whose face should be branded, by Anasuya, Lakshmana's wife who blamed that Chandri had ruined her cousin's married life and was mainly interested in the property and gold of Naranappa, her own maternal uncle's son whose corpse was lying "around like this without even the benefit of a rite" only because of her having distracted him from the path of righteousness. The gold she has been wearing around her neck and wrists should have adorned her sister's body if she were alive—Naranappa's lawful wife—now dead. These comments of the *samskari* men and women place Chandri in her defined caste and social order because of which she has to bear their wrath and venom but if we analyze her role, conduct, intentions, attitudes, actions and impressions on a few characters in the novel step by step, these reveal her to be a grateful, kind, compassionate, humane, refined, cultured woman, in other words a *samskari* human being as compared to the male and female brahmin characters in the novel, who boast of their high birth and *samskars*.

Being a harlot by class and caste, she is the 'other' among the community of upper caste brahmins and hence holds a marginalized status but Naranappa never ill-treated her. He rather defended his living with her and deserting his wife as who would live with a woman who can't give you pleasure. He declared his relations with her justified in the light of such relations of their sages mentioned in the Puranas and other holy texts from which Praneshacharya himself illuminated and explicated the passages describing the beauty of the female body which had made many a sages like Parashara, Vishvamitra, Shankara have illicit sexual union in whom the fellow brahmins took much pride clamouring themselves to be their proud descendents. Though Durgabhatta too (from the smarta brahmin sect considered somewhat lower to Madhva brahmin caste) approved of Naranappa-Chandri relationship in this light but it was not to favour Chandri but only to check and measure "the rival sect's orthodoxy with a questioning eye" whose many members visited the prostitutes quite often. He himself felt jealous of Naranappa for possessing such a beauty resembling the figure of *Matasyagandhi*, "the Fisherwoman in the Ravi Varma print hung up" in his bedroom "shyly trying to hide her breasts bursting through her poor rag of a sari," (8) the foul smelling fisherwoman whose body had become perfumed after her physical union with the sage Parashara. Durgabhatta, like many other middle-aged and young brahmins of this and other agraharas, secretly desired Chandri and he even ogled at her when after Naranappa's death she was standing in a corner, aloof and isolated with her head covered and who seldom moved out of the house when Naranappa was alive. She used to be beautifully clad and adorned her hair with the blooming fragrant flowers of the night queen grown in their backyard whereas the wives of other brahmins wore the withered flowers collected from the temple altar. She dissuaded Naranappa from eating the food cooked by her, eating fish and meat which she could have in the house of Muslims whenever she liked as it was not allowed in his dharma but Naranappa did not bother about these prohibitions, called these "sheer pigheadedness" and shared his food and joy with her. Both of them provided emotional support to each other. Instead of abiding by his discourteous commands in his drunken state to bring liquor for Praneshacharya who had come to advise him in certain matters, she was respectful towards the Acharya and advised Naranappa not to behave improperly.

Thus though Chandri's relationship with Naranappa was not socially approved yet both of them lived happily for ten years as if made for each other. She neither demanded anything from Naranappa nor did she meddle with his other affairs or tried to transgress her caste limits as she was aware of his and her own caste status but she lived and behaved like a cultured woman. The only regret she had from this relationship was that in spite of her staying with Naranappa for ten long years "she still hadn't had a child" and regretted "She had got everything, yet had nothing." (54) She used to think: "If she had borne a son, he could have become a great musician: if a daughter, she could have taught her to dance, classical style." (54) But she was conscious of the fate and plight of the women of her class "ever auspicious, daily-wedded, the one without widowhood." Her desire to be a mother is every woman's natural desire and what is more important is her progressive thinking of educating her children without any discrimination. These were her feelings, thoughts, dreams and desires in relation to Naranappa. Hence though not a legally wedded wife from an upper caste, she is not a money minting prostitute as declared by the brahmin women in the agrahara but a sincere human being who alone along with Praneshacharya is grieved over the demise of Naranappa: "Not a human soul there felt a pang at Naranappa's death, not even women and children." (3) Whereas other *samskari* brahmins are unwilling to perform Naranappa's *samskar* because of many religious and personal reasons based on property disputes, it is only Chandri who is anxious and worried about the plague-hit corpse of Naranappa and wants it to be cremated as per the proper rites to help Naranappa's salvation. "If Naranappa's body didn't get the proper rituals, he could become a tormenting ghost. She had enjoyed life with him for ten years. How could she rest till he got a proper funeral?" (44) "If they didn't give him a death-rite according to the books, he'll surely become an evil spirit." (45)

When the question of meeting the expenses of the funeral obsequies—*Samskara*—is raised, it is she who comes forward, removes all her gold and offers it to Praneshacharya to meet the total expenses for the proper rites of the man who had given her all the comforts and joys." Instead of appreciating her act of offering her gold, the staring at the heap of gold worth two thousand rupees and the quarrel of Durgabhatta and Lakshmana and their wives, Sitadevi and Anasuya (mythical names ironically used) over the possession of this gold (who had earlier warned their husbands, whispering into their ears not to agree in a hurry to perform the rites as the guru will excommunicate them) and now their persuading of their husbands individually to claim before Praneshacharya their rights to cremate the dead body of Naranappa so that Chandri's gold could come to them exposes the hypocrisy, greed, hatred, selfishness and jealousies of these *samskari* brahmins who are expected to be above these base feelings, projects Chandri as a *samskari* human being. It is interesting to observe that now instead of blaming Chandri for Naranappa's pollution, they start accusing each other for their nefarious practices and intentions with regard to Naranappa. "Praneshacharya grew anxious. Why did Chandri spoil everything with her good intentions?" (10) Her act of "compassion—the human gold—which Chandri evinced by offering her ornaments was not found either in the Acharya or in his brahmin society. Chandri's offer of gold was an act of faith in man which the agrahara could not project in a crisis. Her gold only exposed the vacuity of the order." (Sundari: 68). Praneshacharya is moved by this act of her, appreciates it before his invalid wife, Bhagirathi, "how pure Chandri's heart was, how she laid down all her gold and what new complications arose from that generous act." (20)When the night falls he asks Chandri to take rest in the dining-room of his house, gives her a mat, a pillow and a blanket to sleep comfortably and also returns her gold saying, "Naranappa is dead. But you've your life to live." (49) It is Praneshacharya alone who is compassionate towards her in her distress and she also finds only in him the support after Naranappa.

Another act of Chandri which projects her as a better human being vis-a-vis the brahmin community of Durvasapura is her following the Acharya, to avoid the anger of brahmins, when not finding answer to Naranappa's cremation in the Books of Law he had gone to the Maruti temple to seek the answer for this dilemma so that the brahmins could cremate the dead body and take food. She carries plantains in the corner of her sari, waits for him under a tree. She is full of pity and compassion for this man who is suffering for others. She remembers the words of her mother who used to say, "prostitutes should get pregnant by such holy men" and realizes, "Such a man was Acharya, he had such virtues; he glowed. But one had to be lucky to be blessed by such people," (46) though she has no intention of entrapping him. On

Acharya's coming back from the temple without finding any answer, she follows him in the darkness, falls at his feet for seeking his blessings, and while lifting her up he feels the warmth of her body and full breasts. Chandri holds him down, gives him the plantains to eat and caresses him. This tender love leads them to have sexual union. When Acharya wakes up in the midnight: "His head was in Chandri's lap. His cheek was pressed into her low naked belly. Chandri's fingers caressed his back, his ears, his head." (67) He feels himself fallen but does not "scold" or "despise" her for this. Rather he tells her that now he had lost the authority to decide for the agrahara. He asks her that this act must be confessed before the agrahara gathering and they must tell "this happened." "If I don't have the courage to speak, tomorrow you must speak out. I'm ready to do the funeral rites myself. I've no authority to tell any other brahmin to do them, that's all." She lets him go ahead and reaching the agrahara goes to the room where Naranappa's rotting, stinking body is lying and considers it her duty to cremate it. "That's not her lover Naranappa. It's neither brahmin nor shudra. A carcass. A stinking rotting carcass" (70), over which so much fuss was being created. Gathering courage, she goes alone in the night to the cartman Sheshappa's house and on his refusal to meddle with "a brahmin corpse" she seeks the help of a Muslim fish merchant Ahmad Bari (an outcaste), a friend of Naranappa whom he had helped with a small loan to buy oxen when he was bankrupt, to cremate the dead body in the dark of night with the firewood lying in her house (nobody knows about this fact and the *samskari* brahmins including Praneshacharya keep on wriggling over the ritual sanctities foolishly). Through this third humane act, she breaks the tradition and caste barriers like Naranappa and "gets the better of Praneshacharya: she takes the burden off the Brahmin's hands, but exposes the inhumanity of orthodox Brahminism that permitted itself to be trapped in ritual hairsplitting when faced with life-and-death issues" (Parthasarthy: 195-96). After cremation, she weeps to her heart's desire for Naranappa, collects her clothes, money and gold and leaves in the dark to travel by road to catch a bus in the morning for Kundapura without even informing Praneshacharya about the cremation and her intention to depart. Instead of taking advantage of the situation to blackmail Praneshacharya and see Praneshacharya's humiliation in front of others if he spoke about the last night's act, her decision to leave the place quietly speaks of her good *samskars* as compared to those of Praneshacharya's *samskari* fellow brahmins who would have left no stone unturned to downgrade him on knowing his inadvertent act. Her decision of not meeting him before leaving as it would make such a noble man feel small before her, too is an indicator of her greatness as a human being and regard for the genuine goodness of the Acharya and his kindness towards her throughout. Thus we see that Chandri's belonging to a lower caste in no way makes her a base and lower human being, Rather she possesses the basic human quality "Compassion, the right way of dharma, being human brahminhood." (48) P. Usha Sundari has very appropriately summed up her qualities, how *samskrta*, refined and cultured she is:

> she has a conscience that is lovable. At least, she is not thankless. she wants the funeral rites to be performed for the separated man, with whom she had spent a good many intimate moments. The money paid or the ornaments gifted, do not compensate the feelings, however fake or rehearsed. She is the only person who demonstrates man's love for man. She does not pack up or go to her village (Kundapura) the moment Naranappa dies. Rather she offers all her gold for the *Samskara* of her man. She is another Antigone running towards uncertainties for certain basic values She goes back as she came, somewhat mellower perhaps, but never richer. Before she goes, however, she trounces the acharya's pride." (Sundari: 72)

Though Chandri leaves the stage at this point right in the middle of the text and we are not told of her whereabouts afterwards but the impact she leaves on the mind of Praneshacharya (he could not have the courage to tell the fellow brahmins the truth) after exposing him to the world of flesh, which he had not explored and tasted so far because of his choice marriage with an invalid woman which would keep him away from the lust, and his asceticism and service of her will surely guarantee him a seat in heaven, leaves him in further dilemma, conflict and turmoil which have been shown through a series of interior monologues of the Acharya in the second half of the novel. He starts realizing the duplicity in his life and feels himself "Hung—suspended under two truths like 'Trishanku.'" (92) His contact with Chandri now makes him aware of the difference between the world of beauty and ugliness and he understands the willing submission of the ancient sages of the Hindu mythology and that of his studious ashram friend Mahabala and of Naranappa to the female beauty. He also finds Naranappa having a victory over him who had earlier challenged him. Chandri, thus is present with Praneshacharya even through her absence. His strenuous struggle with himself while passing through the world of real life experiences in the company of Putta in their beauty, ugliness and ruthlessness, resolving to own the responsibility of his action boldly and his reaching the decision of living with Chandri openly like Naranappa as this way he will "remake" himself as a human being show him now a reborn person "a trija, thrice born," have been pictured very incisively which may be called the dilemma of everyman of Praneshacharya's kind of mental make up and social status in the given socio-cultural milieu. The shift of ethics from the socialistic and religious to existentialism is quite prominent from this stage. (Bhat: 7)

Chandri thus has ushered him to the world of flesh and he is so overpowered with the passion and lust that he pines to caress her breasts and even those of the lowcaste sweeper girl, Belli (who is used off and on by Shripati, Lakshmana's son-in-law, whose wife Lilavati denied him physical pleasure as a punishment on her mother's advice, the formula she had applied on her husband also) and any other young woman. Even the full breasts and thighs of Padmavati, the harlot, he was introduced to by Putta to spend a night with her, fascinate him and stir in him the fires of passion but he does not go cheap to satisfy his lust with them. The question that arises here is whether he wants to go to

Chandri only for sexual pleasure or her qualities as a noble human being too attract him which he had been appreciating earlier. Maybe now he wants to live the life of a perfect householder enjoying the life of pleasure while doing his duties and raising children, the desire for a son had also arisen in him while accompanying Putta, and in Chandri alone he visualizes such a partner with whom he can settle a home which his wife had also desired him to do when she was alive. So the desire of Praneshacharya for Chandri indirectly presents her in a good light. Even Shripati talks very high of her qualities in front of the members of the drama troupe:

> Whatever anybody may say, whatever brahmins bray—I swear—what do you say?—in a hundred-mile radius is there any woman as lovely, as bright, as good, as Chandri? Take a count. If you find one, I'll give up my caste. What does it matter if she's a whore? You tell me, didn't she behave better than any wife with Naranappa? If he drank too much and vomited, she wiped up the mess. She even wiped ours up, didn't she? Anytime, even at midnight, when he woke her up she cooked and served him, all smiles. Which brahmin woman would do so much? Stupid shaven widows! (72)

As compared to the jealous and greedy wives of the brahmins and other women of lowcaste it is Chandri who stands apart for her praiseworthy traits which undoubtedly make her a *samskari* woman in spite of her belonging to a low caste.

Thus we see that being a subaltern in that social set up though she cannot speak openly and assert her opinion of right and wrong but she speaks through her good-intentioned acts which cross the boundary of caste-laid norms. Through her humane acts Anantha Murthy as "a critical insider" not only lays bare the hypocrisy and shams of the decadent brahminic order but by making Praneshacharya ultimately decide to confess his act fearlessly before the brahmins, cremate the dead body of Naranappa himself (What an irony of human perception!), go to Kundapura, start living with Chandri openly, he also floats his reformative vision of the rehabilitation of the prostitutes like

Chandri who are the product and victims of the patriarchal and rigid caste system. If the learned religious men take lead in this connection, the victimization of the women of this class will surely end. Moreover, the offspring born out of the union of such a noble and educated man and such a cultured woman will surely write a bright future for any cultural set-up. The reference to the sage Parashara, the great ascetic from whose sexual union with a fish wife was born Vyasa, the seer, the compiler of the Vedas and the epic poet of the *Mahabharata*, is suggestive of such a birth from the womb of Chandri as she has carried the seed of Praneshacharya. But whether Praneshacharya will have the courage to go to Kundapura by breaking the tight shackles of the *Samskaras* of his caste, own Chandri and her child socially and legally or will he just keep her as a keep like Naranappa or Mahabala is a question mark because in the end of the narrative he is shown still grappling with himself: "How can I face all those brahmins alone?" (137) The "anxious, expectant" Praneshacharya sits in the lorry going to Durvasapuram and the narrative itself ends with a question mark: "He will travel, for another four or five hours. Then, after that, what?" Thus we find that "while narrating this tale, the author raises several questions and highlights various conflicts and contrasts in society, but it ends without offering any specific solution. Indeed, it confirms that there is no specific solution" (*Samskara*, a Book Review, Meghdutam com.).

The narrative which contains so many questions one after the other, through the portrayal of the *samskars* of Chandri's intentions, conduct and acts poses many other pertinent questions also before the orthodox caste-based patriarchal system. Who is responsible for the making of prostitutes? Is being born in a family of prostitutes a girl's fault? Does a prostitute's daughter have no right to lead a respectable married life? Should a prostitute's daughter also become a prostitute? Is the formation of prostitutes their own choice or is it a part of the plan of Destiny or the creation of patriarchal system or the result of the failure of the institution of marriage which the bard in William Blake's poem "London" refers to?

How the youthful harlot's curse
Blasts the newborn infant's tear,
And blights with plagues the marriage hearse. (36)

Is once a brahmin always a brahmin? The social and religious orders need to find answers to these and many more such questions and redefine their values of purity and impurity to put an end to the institution of prostitution and rehabilitate the women of this class with dignity. But to the two questions (i) who is a true *samskari*? (ii) does your birth or caste determine your *Samskaras* or your humane attitudes and actions? there cannot be two answers. The latter question implies the most probable answer to the problematic taken up in this paper.

Works Cited

Bakhtin, Mikhail, *Problems of Dostoevsky's Poetics*. Trans. and ed. Caryl Emerson. Manchester: Manchester University Press, 1984.

Bhat, Sharda V, "Shift in Ethics in U.R. Anantha Murthy's *Samskara*," *Indian Journal of Contemporary English Criticism*, ed. Mandal B. Beg, Vol. 1, No. I, Jan.-June 2002, pp. 5-9.

Blake, William, *Songs of Innocence and Songs of Experience*, ed. A.M. Wilkinson. London: University Tutorial Press, 1958.

Derrida, Jacques, "Structure, sign and play in the discourse of human sciences," *Modern Criticism and Theory: A Reader*, ed. David Lodge. Longman: London and New York, 1988, pp. 108-23.

Murthy, U.R. Anantha, *Samskara*. Oxford University Press, 1978 .

Parthasarthy, Rajagopal, "*Samskara*: The Passing of the Brahmin Tradition," *Masterpieces of Asian Literature in Comparative Perspective*, ed. Barbara Stoler Miller. New York: M.E. Sharpe, pp. 189-200.

Samskara, a Book Review, Meghdutam.com.

Sundari, Usha, "Ritual to Paranoia: A Study of Anantha Murthy's *Samskara*," *Indian Journal of Contemporary English Criticism*, ed. Mandal B. Beg, Vol. I, No. I, Jan.-June 2002, pp. 64-74.

Labyrinths in *Samskara*

SANJOY SAKSENA
Allahabad University

Though *Samskara* has been subtitled A *Rite for a Dead Man* it has been defined as 'realizing of past perceptions' and should be understood as such not merely in its restricted sense as funeral rites. When one looks back after reading the novel, one is struck by the text's preoccupation with Brahminism and sub-human underpinning of the outcaste characters. These subaltern are mostly women and their marginalization in the novel is the result of the Brahmin society's obsession with itself. The pressures of the changing times work on the Brahmins but the *sudras* or out-castes are never allotted their due share in the social set up nor is there any effort made to redeem their plight. Thus, the novel is and remains primarily a Brahmin text. In the Afterword, A.K. Ramanujan talks about 'questions without answers.' One question that arises in the mind over and over again is as to why the outcastes are not given a more central position in the novel and why do they remain shallow caricatures? Is it because it's a novel written by a Brahmin and mainly for a Brahmin readership, for the *sudras*, at the time it was written, had little access to education? In the good old days, including the period the novel deals with, outcastes were by and large unacceptable in schools and colleges. The sacred texts with which Praneshacharya is constantly preoccupied were deliberately kept away from them. It is little surprise that they were always treated unfairly in treatises that dealt with mythologies, codes of conduct, and religious practices. A subaltern had no say, was unable to express his point of view or find a representation that was beyond patronizing, in the religious texts or other discursive practices. The marginalization of the *sudras* is in-built in the very conception and mechanics of the novel. It is expressly about Brahmins and by a Brahmin who is worried about his decaying community. The decline of the Brahmins is throughout linked with half-castes and it is these lesser mortals in the Brahmin eye that are responsible for the destruction of their purity. *Samskara* also involves tradition that one has inherited from one's ancestors and it is these traditions or *Samskaras* that Praneshacharya stands for. Even Naranappa was a peculiar by-product of these traditions—he had imbibed the brahminical way of life and prayer from his parents that he gives up after the death of his wife.

In the novel it is not as much he as Chandri who is blamed for having spoilt him and defiled the entire Madhva community. The destruction of *Samskaras* is therefore blamed on the corrupt lower castes and the ignorant subalterns. The sweep of the novel is such that the entire moral degradation is pinned on those who are placed lower down in the caste hierarchy. The point that is missed is that the purest of the pure Brahmins themselves invite trouble for themselves because they tried to practise ideals that were no longer sustainable, partially because they were based on unscientific thought and partly because they are too difficult to practice in a world where existence itself was becoming a problem. In the novel we see the Brahmins as having lofty ideals but in practice they suffer from all human weaknesses and failings. Contact with the lower classes exposes the inhumanity that underlies religion where the quintessence of humanism is overruled by taboos and dogmas. It is not so much the fall of high caste Brahmins from the expectations that their religion has from them but their failure to observe basic human obligations like disposing off a rotting dead body that is shocking. And their reading and understanding of religion prevents them from performing their duties towards a man they had not only known themselves but had been connected to through their ancestors. They eye the gold that his low-born mistress was willing to part with to pay for the funeral expenses and to whet the majority's appetite for rituals. Gold in whosoever's hands it may go remains unpolluted for them but the owner's dead body is unworthy of even being disposed off.

> The women calculated swiftly: heaps of gold was worth at least two thousand rupees. One after another, the wives scanned their

> husbands' faces. The Brahmins bowed their heads: they were afraid, fearful that the lust for gold might destroy Brahmin purity. But in the mind of every one of them flashed the question: if some other Brahmin should perform the final rite for Naranappa, he might lose his brahminhood and yet put all the gold on his wife's neck. (10)

The bait is tempting but never recognized as a bait and therefore efforts are made to secure the gold without being caught on the wrong foot. The act of participating in the cremation they think would ruin their purity and lead to damnation. But the property that Naranappa owned and lived in becomes a matter of dispute among the Brahmins; religion cannot stop them from acting clever. This shows that the character of the Brahmins was flawed and duplicitous largely due to their religious beliefs. Religion ironically instead of uplifting them spiritually and morally contributes and abets in their dehumanization.

The great Hindu faith had been understood by them with scholastic pains in such a manner that they ironically fail as human beings. And for this the lower castes cannot be blamed in the novel or can be blamed elsewhere. The point is that lower castes, be it Chandri, Belli or Putta, only contribute towards exposing their weaknesses of character and in no way degrade it themselves. The novel itself is supposed to be about a decadent Brahmin community that finds its women unappealing and devoid of sexuality. Madhva women of the agrahara as Anantha Murthy paints them seem to be too plain and ordinary for their men folk. They are depicted as being pure, religious, quarrelsome, garrulous, greedy, superstitious, lacking in feminine graces and patriarchy driven. They do not desire to do anything that would upset the traditional notions of a proper and virtuous life.

The women characters have been victimized by patriarchy to such an extent that they speak the language of patriarchy and do not even spare their own subaltern sisters. If the subaltern women are seen in poor light it is because the entire society, men, women and children, connive against them. Therefore, both Chandri and Belli resort to a politics of survival in which their sexuality is perhaps their finest weapon. They share the beliefs of the Madhva community because they have been raised in a manner that stamps out assertion against the Brahmins and yet are the ones who pose the most serious threat to brahminism by merely coming into intimate contact with the supposedly pious and noble males. The lower caste subaltern women, Chandri and Belli, use the men folk under the spell of their sexuality against the higher caste women to save themselves from any additional burden of the working of social authority on them. These subaltern women succeed in the novel in destabilizing the Madhva society which is biased against them, their original sin being birth in the lower rungs of the caste ridden social ladder. Chandri and Belli are sexually exploited and while they allow their sexual exploitation, it is not permitted to happen without their exploiting the males to their advantage. The sexual equations that are formed are intriguing and masculinity is made to work against itself to benefit the subalterns. In this psychic and sexual battle of low born women, it is the high born males who are emotionally traumatized and led to searching existential questions that shake their roots—the traditions and myths that sustain them are put to test as much as the people themselves. The question that one might well ask is: if subaltern women have been using their sexuality to subvert the caste ridden social system, how is it that it continues to function even till this day, and how does it fight back?

One could say that these subaltern women who strive against their exploitation share the same value system in which their arch enemies the Madhva Brahmins are advantageously placed. They subscribe to the same kind of myths that place the Brahmins at a high pedestal and the lower castes down below. The doctrines of *dharma* and *karma* go against the subalterns and yet they do not challenge them. The subalterns, due to lack of education and centuries of serfdom, have been deprived of the ability to challenge the beliefs on a rational and intellectual plane. Their threat to the system of beliefs is expediential and not systematic. Chandri resorts to her extreme decision of inviting the Muslims to cremate Naranappa when she sees the body of her beloved getting decomposed in the hut. The Brahmins do not listen to her and Praneshacharya does not have the gumption to go against whatever his caste ridden fidgety conscience and fellow Brahmins have to say. She does not hang on in the agrahara but disappears without leaving a clue about her whereabouts. And it is not without an acute sense of guilt that she has the cremation performed. Her disappearance and Praneshacharya's being left in the lurch in a state of expectancy gives strength to those who are not guided by any higher principles. The caste system, as one sees it in the novel, has always received jolts and then returned to its former position, has survived.

If meaning is plural then the novel supports more than one, certainly, submits to another meaning that is against its grain, making its structure and weave work against itself. The central personality Praneshacharya if pushed aside, which the novel resists, yields a different picture altogether. The downplaying of this picture that consists of the subaltern women by the author makes it alarming—opens discursive structures of subjectivity that are concealed in *Samskara.* These marginal women have been deprived of language—language that is governed by regimes of social power and from whom Anantha Murthy is not free. The silence of these women is the result of the working of knowledge and power in Kannada society. Though it is definitely a sign of their inferiority and helplessness, it is also threatening because their being silenced by social forces indicates the threat they pose to the production and maintenance of existing power relations. Seduced by their sexuality, the Brahmin males detest their own women and cause implosions within their own community. These women, who are marginal, bring about a change in the consciousness of highborn men. They get exploited because they are economically crippled and politically weak and it is in the process of exploitation that they become so close to the Brahmin menfolk that they start subverting the rules of existence that should be practised according to the dominant Madhva community.

We often tend to apply those standards for judging the novel which the culture that has bred it produces. These standards may not be acceptable any longer. To focus on the transcendental plane is often to miss the point of the novel and in this connive the overarching fetishized myths. A radical critique may become a necessity in this case and to make it possible it becomes obligatory to position oneself outside the Kannada culture of the 1930s which but for minor changes continues to flourish to this day. Failure of the Brahmins to locate the negativity of their milieu from within their own socio-religious system is too obvious. Subalterns have a micro-logical relationship with the Brahmin society that is based on their exploitation and the bonds of humanity that bind them are simply too thin. Putta is a happy-go-lucky man who does not have much problems in adjusting to his position in the caste ridden society but he understands his own limitations that his low caste has imposed. Such limitations and restrictions thwart all his chances of doing better and at the bottom of it all lies his reconciliation but in no way does he accept his lot for he talks about his hybridity—being the offspring of a Brahmin through a subaltern woman.

The clash between Praneshacharya's consciousness and the socio-religious processes that follow the death of Naranappa open doors for a critique. The estrangement of the reader from an unusual situation provides the much-needed critical distance and a dissonant ground for social criticism. The cultural dialectic that the novel supports is one between Naranappa and the Brahminical social mores of which Praneshacharya is the most respectable champion in his village. Naranappa knows that his binary opposite was Praneshacharya and he had taken upon himself to finish Praneshacharya because the values that Praneshacharya symbolized went against him:

> Let me see who wins in the end—you or me. I'll destroy brahminism, I certainly will. My only sorrow is that there's no brahminism really left to destroy in this place—except you. (23)

In the novel, the foremost question for the caste ridden reader becomes one of preserving his own centuries old values—one of saving his own hardened self—sanctified by the wisdom of the great sages and lawgivers. The point that deserves to be noted is that in the conflict the lower classes get marginalized, specially the women and deserve to be foregrounded. The critic is also shaped by the society that he seeks to criticize and his criticism that is supposed to be impartial actually can be located within the society's preferences that he tries to differ with and can be predicated on a situation that he tries to escape. Being a part and product of the society he seeks to critique makes him vulnerable and suspect because to claim freedom from class interests and caste moorings is one thing and to attain it is another. It is this paradox that makes the subaltern position within the novel tricky and troublesome. Even the critic who claims critical distance and the capacity to negotiate the dialectic of upper caste and lower caste can be trapped in a slippery terrain. Why should Chandri have been merely a mistress to Naranappa and not his lawfully wedded wife? The rhetorical answer is that it is more caste than class. It is in the light of this fact that we can infer that for all his free thinking even the widower Naranappa is not above caste. In such an event, perhaps the safest position would be to look for fissures within the structures of the novel and the society it seeks to discuss and address. If not anything else this should provide for a radical perspective.

In the entire novel, caste assumes central importance. The caste system is by common consensus the world's longest surviving hierarchy and is based on the principles of purity and superiority, qualities that one is supposed to inherit by birth. A person becomes a member of a particular caste with his birth and dies in it. The *dalits* or lowcastes are outside the caste system and their exploitation is common throughout India. They are looked down upon because of their low caste; birth in a low caste is supposed to be the result of their bad deeds or *karma* in previous lives. The caste system has been recognized by all sane Hindus as pernicious and deserves to be abolished, yet it flourishes due to the hold of racial purity on our minds. If caste system had been done away with, Naranappa would have been given a decent funeral and Praneshacharya would not have had as close an encounter with Chandri as he had, may not have been mentally and spiritually destabilized so as to engender a tragedy. Praneshacharya's tragedy too is a tragedy if we analyze it from within the Hindu caste system or else he could have easily married Chandri following his wife's death and Chandri, interestingly enough, would be twice married as it happens in more open western societies. Therefore, throughout the novel, caste remains the defining feature of *Samskara* and its shadow continues to hang on all the characters, ever after, because the novel is open-ended. Not one character in the entire novel can think beyond caste nor can he or she, being ill equipped intellectually and emotionally, attempt to destroy it. All men and women are the products of the caste system and its victims, though it must be conceded that some thrive on it. Caste system has survived because of the security that it sometimes provides people locked within its cocoon. Even the Brahmins who are the apex within the caste system have to suffer because of the sacrifices that they have to make and the restricting obligations that they have to fulfill. It is in order to save their caste that they compromise with their basic independence and their proclivities toward more liberal and universal human values that are out of compulsions seen from within the confines of caste. Even salvation is related to caste and the religious practices that accompany it. The purer Brahmins would not associate themselves with the lower castes for fear of damnation and eternal perdition—of being created in the lives to come as lesser forms of life.

The novel is definitely male with hardly any pretence of gynocentricism or with female sympathies. It is the internalization of patriarchal values and Brahminism that moves all the characters. Neither Chandri nor Praneshacharya know their way out after violation of the norms of their society. After performing the cremation with the aid of Muslims, she does not know where to go and Praneshacharya after sleeping with her launches himself on an existential trail. The point is that both continue to think from within the tyrannical Hindu-brahminical system and are unable to break themselves free. In the struggle for autonomy, Chandri and Naranappa were more successful whereas Praneshacharya moves forwards and backwards. Whatever success Chandri and Naranappa achieve is to a large extent the consequence of being pushed out of the brahminic brotherhood by the adherents of conservative Brahminism.

All characters adore the Hindu faith, they think and function from within Hinduism and that which they adore becomes the author of their own woes, as the faith demands rigid adherence from its followers. Chandri has advantages too because of her low caste compared to the Brahmins who do not expect her to follow complicated, involved and involving religious guidelines that are supposed to be beyond her comprehension. Her inability to understand the nuances and depths of Hindu-brahminical thought makes it easier for her to violate the sanctified norms. She does what Praneshacharya could not have dared to do or imagine because of his strong religious moorings: Naranappa's cremation with the aid of Muslims. Her daring does not necessitate a reform which Praneshacharya's decision could have. It calls for criticism from all quarters, least of all, provide food for thought on humanistic lines. Praneshacharya, throughout the novel, does not abandon his faith in his religion, its beliefs and practices nor does he get the opportunity to approve of Chandri's extreme action. This can be understood if we judge from within Hinduism.

The novel from the feminist point of view appears warped and as one that completely belies women's hopes and aspirations. It even invites the temptation to straighten male prejudices that are at work, to counter social reality that is nothing but a patriarchal construction. Nowhere in the novel do we hear of the real feelings of Chandri, Belli, Bhagirathi, or Sitadevi. Their inscapes seem to be unimportant. We do not know what they thought of the Brahmin men nor do we know whether they felt exploited even at the hands of Praneshacharya because for all his goodness he does represent patriarchalism and parasitic Brahminism. The women, especially upper caste women, do not attack the social system based on hierarchies but try to make the most from within its confines to their advantage even though they meet with resistance, amusingly from their husbands and other male relatives. Brahmin male's fondness for the subaltern women is basically sexual gratification and a cruel weakness which involves helplessness, exploitation and pain for the hapless females. Anantha Murthy ignores the psychosexual trauma that these women had to endure: it was not important enough for him and its occurrence it seems is taken for granted. It is almost as though these women do not think about their sexual harassment. Crimes against subaltern women go unreported and are hardly considered seriously for it is they who are blamed for problems that have been inflicted on them. That a Brahmin male should have made sexually explicit gestures is not taken note of, least of all condemned, and the shame lies not so much in the vulgarity of such gestures but in the fear of being polluted. If *Samskara* is a testimony to the prevailing social reality and has something to do with social change, which it has, then, it pushes women into the well of patriarchal mess—situations that have no real answers (within the novel) to their problems. If the answers must come from women, then, the novel by providing them little space, does not help very much. If we consider the novel as being a part and product of the social set-up, then it is a victim of the prevailing social evils and does not provide impetus to those looking for progressive answers. Those who are trapped inside the villages and agraharas of India are hardly given the opportunity to become aware of their plight, this perhaps is more so, because the ostensible focus of the novel is Praneshacharya's consciousness that is reinforced by the powerful and recurrent use of socially sanctified myths.

Gynocentric myths are relegated into the background or made to serve the patriarchy by clever and perverse interpretations. The goddesses are so utilized by Brahminism that they make the women more firmly entangled within the patriarchal web. Even Naranappa's arguments for leading the kind of existence that he enjoys with Chandri are also self-centredly patriarchal. The contradiction that they contain is that while they justify his own indulgences, they are at the same time against women's dignity. It is this that makes his unconventional ideas powerless and dogmatic shared thoughts prevail. His consciousness therefore to the Indian mind appears more idiosyncratic and less convincing. Naranappa's phallocentricism nullifies his progressiveness, renders him socially impotent. His ill taken advice given under the influence of liquor was ironically to have a grain of truth for Praneshacharya:

> 'You read those lush sexy Puranas, but you preach a life of barrenness. But my words, they say what they mean: if I say sleep with a woman, it means sleep with a woman; if I say eat fish, it means eat fish. Can I give you brahmins a piece of advice, Acharya-re? Push those sickly wives of yours into the river. Be like the sages of your

> holy legends—get hold of a fish-scented Fisherwoman who can cook you fish soup, and go to sleep in her arms. And if you don't experience god when you wake up, my name isn't Naranappa.' Then he quaffed his liquor in his cup and let out a long belch. (26)

Such pieces of counsel do not go well with Praneshacharya whose sickly wife is also ridiculed. Be as it may, he does appear seductive to the young males scared of a life of abstinence, spiritual pursuits, and restraint that their noble birth inflicts on them. Such notions the youth found soul destroying and Naranappa's supposedly deviant advices were soulful to them. The Brahmins are people in search of greater and higher truth—a truth based on the doctrines of the transmigration of the soul and painful notions of purity that would yield dividends in the lives to come. To them dissidence amounts to questioning the very end and purpose of their lives, an existential problem that seems to lead nowhere because it does not have religious sanction. Violation of religion tantamounts to violation of life and ensuring a place for oneself in hell.

To repudiate such a philosophy was to go back on all that one had believed in and for the Brahmins this was more of a spiritual problem and less of a social one. In the conflict between individual consciousness and the shared value system a poetry may be born but the chances of an alternate system of beliefs, more correct and 'truer truths,' emerging appears bleak. Therefore, the lives of such diverse personalities as Praneshacharya and Naranappa can never serve as role models for village people caught up in the uncomfortable drift towards modernity. They, at best, bring about a catharsis through their destruction. And these moments of catharsis for the feminists become moments of castration when the principal phallocentric figure comes crashing to the ground like a giant tree shaking up the area around. The success of the feminine lies in its power to destroy those who emblematize patriarchy and Brahmin made notions of sexuality. After Naranappa's funeral Chandri leaves the agrahara for she does not know the paths her life would take and similarly Praneshacharya leaves the village after an intimate encounter with her not knowing what to expect in life: one is lost in her victory, another in his defeat. Both are at the threshold of a new life, waiting for chance and destiny to come to their rescue.

Women's hysteria in the novel shows their refusal to accept things as they are and their reluctant acceptance of the prevailing tradition: they assert their position and then succumb. Sitadevi goes crazy at the thought of losing Naranappa gold and Lakshmidevamma is furious with the brahmins. Hysteria is anger, protest and helplessness, at once. It is through hysteria that they attack the system and then try to prove their point. Even in their marginality through hysteria they manage to raise questions that trouble the male dominated social order. Driven by personal and caste considerations, women direct their hysteria against each other as well.

Samskara is about Brahmins and the subalterns struggling in the ebb and flow of social change that transition towards modernity has brought about. It is about this transitory phase in the life of the agrahara that Anantha Murthy tries to capture the pangs of spiritual evolution and the severe emotional and spiritual crisis. The clashes between people as also values is autocriticism that the village society indulges in and it is this that disturbs their peace. The Brahmin world is the world of the petty bourgeoisie of the 1930s trying to adapt itself, with an eye on the past and the hoary traditions that sustained them, to the changing social structures. Anantha Murthy himself is a product of these social structures and the novel itself has been described as a bourgeoisie form of writing. Therefore, to expect that the subalterns, especially women among them, would find the space that they deserve is to belie one's expectations and it becomes incumbent on the critics to raise the issue—discover wherever they are absent or present as an under text in the textual palimpsest. It becomes necessary to place the women and subalterns within the petty bourgeoisie male tradition and locate how they accept and disrupt it, simultaneously, thereby creating a dialectic that must go on—read the silences and the meanings that surround them. In the polyphony of the text the muffled voices cannot be allowed to be lost. For the senile and half-wit Lakshmidevamma is insignificant in the larger scheme of things. She is ignored and bypassed by all the learned Brahmins and yet it is she who comes out with the sanest advice for the entire lot. Lakshmidevamma abuses profusely, specially Garuda for having stolen "a poor old shaven widow's money," and as she belches she utters just the right words by way of counsel and indictment:

> Where has your Brahminism gone, you rascals! Don't you know you'll fall into the lowest hell reserved for outcastes and perish there? In this agrahara, in all my born days, have I have seen a body kept uncremated all night? Not once. Rama, Rama, the times are rotten, rotten. Brahminism is in ruins. Why don't you shave your heads and become Muslims, why do you need to be Brahmins, you! (43)

Anantha Murthy's oeuvre in *Samskara* is essentially male, one could allege, patriarchal, narcissistic. This patriarchal or phallic narcissism subverts the possibilities of the novel to throw up a woman's vision that has to be analytically derived and deduced, even coaxed. This limited vision results in male phantasms that are stale, clichéd and weary. Therefore, it becomes necessary to locate the fissures in the text and look for that which has been concealed and trivialized behind the *purdah* of a high caste man's vision. Women in the novel become victims of an unconscious resistance from the author and it is this that provokes the social conscience. They become victims of sexual politics and the norms of a society run on the guidelines it has inherited from a patriarchal past and religion. Chandri's recapitulation after the cremation and her guilt deprive her from the privilege of making any real onslaught on the social text. She does what she herself thinks she should not have done and loads the dice against herself. She undoes what she could have done: forced a humanist reform through her action. In the economy of control Chandri is nowhere and her attempts to manipulate situations through the use of her sexuality do not yield desired results. Praneshacharya does not arrive at any precise conclusion about the last rites of Naranappa nor does he in any way attempt to get even a semblance of respectability for her in society. The feelings that he has for her remain throughout illegitimate desires, those he himself would not give sanction to.

Praneshacharya is the man in the Madhva agrahara who possesses the authority to give religious and social meaning—he is the one who holds the key to the logos. His venerated rationality is such that for Naranappa's cremation he goes to the Maruti temple and places a flower each on the god's both shoulders. The flower that would fall first would decide the fate of the rotting corpse and this quirk is to become the rationale behind his decision making and wisdom. He is scared of women and considers them to be objects of perverse desire that are to be shunned. His marrying a cripple and nursing her at one level shows his kind nature but deprivation of a normal and natural life renders him an incomplete man. Women in his eyes continue to be an enigma: he miserably fails to understand Chandri and is befuddled and besotted by her sexuality. He searches for her but never does he approve of his own behaviour nor does he agree with all that Chandri stands for—cleverness and hedonism. Chandri is a forbidden luxury, but elemental, that he had voluntarily denied himself in life. It is the element of guilt that thwarts and frustrates all possibility of the novel serving a large social purpose and the discourse that emanates from it crumbles under the weight of the contradictions that are in-built in it. Women continue to be subservient characters and there is no escape from the depressing religio-social crisis that engulfs them.

The voices of women are weak and incoherent babble, the opposite of rational discourse. The point is that whereas they are supposed to be irrational and not worthy of any serious attention; the towering personality remains an object of awe and highest respect. Praneshacharya does not fall in others' eyes, his stature remains undiminished, and our sympathies remain with him as they would with a Greek tragic hero. His reason does not appear to be a tragic flaw at all in the general scheme of things in the novel. Praneshacharya's logic is based on other worldly and mysterious rationale of religion and his methods of arriving at his conclusions, as he does much to the approval of the other Brahmins of the agrahara and surrounding areas, are at times based on blind chance: placing of flowers on Maruti's both shoulders. But, within the novel, only the women come under attack and Praneshacharya is venerated for believing in obscurantism. This presumptuous understanding of the Hindu faith produces a false consciousness that goes against women and subalterns, leads the hierarchy to gain mastery and control of the ostensibly recalcitrant others. Naranappa's logic that is based on his discrete understanding of the selected myths and Hindu treatises is treated as a false consciousness even though it presents a radical understanding of the Hindu view of life and is definitely more modern and broadminded. Any logic that goes against the established order and its norms or is inimical to its chosen ends becomes an object that has to be attacked. Whatever Naranappa says is subordinated by the Brahmins by pointing an accusing finger at his philistinism and disregard for sanctioned behaviour for the Madhva males. His engagements are never refuted with counter logic but merely brushed aside and condemned. Altruism is never allowed to become an issue nor does the debate take a humanistic drift. Matters are always seen through the selective lens of religion and that Hindu religion which is consistent with Brahminism. Praneshacharya's thinking undergoes a sea-change after his experiences with Chandri. His single track mind starts seeing not just the light of God but shades that are inescapable for ordinary mortals. It is his acceptance of the more controversial side of life that his religion negates and his subsequent attempts to come to grips with his own situation that makes him a truly credible character; it is the honesty with which he tries to come to grapple with his own inner self that makes him a likable personality. After all he did indulge in sexual activities that neither his station in the Madhva community nor his religion could ever approve. In our eyes he does not fall as a man because he doesn't try to cheat himself with falsehoods: "He remembered the first maxim of yoga, 'Yoga is the stilling of the waves of the mind.' 'But No!' he said to himself. 'Put aside even the consolations of recitations and God's holy names, stand alone,' he said to himself. May the mind be like the patterns of light and shade, the forms the branching trees give naturally to sunshine, light in the sky, shadow under the trees, patterns on the ground. If, luckily, there's spray of water—rainbows. May one's life be that sunshine. A mere awareness, a sheer astonishment, still, floating still and self-content, like the sacred Brahmini-kite in the sky." (91)

There is a clear shift in thought, from a quest of rigid and painful morality to an acceptance of the many hues that life can take without forewarnings. The pulls are so strong in different directions that his personality itself is split. Praneshacharya does not give up hope of redemption. Instead of public morality, his standards of judging himself would be privately moral in an amoral world. His failings are the failings of ordinary mortals who are made physiologically and psychologically in such a way that sex sometimes overpowers them. Culture and civilization nowhere on earth permit licentiousness and we are bound by our own society's codes of conduct, therefore, the guilt. Having led a life of great restraint in the service of his community and religion, he associates his sexual propensities with violence and conflict. He thinks his religion had answers to his problems and a solution for his spiritual regeneration. But the answers must come from within the individual. Human problems have human solutions where the other-worldly ideas don't work well. Conflict in his divergent selves that had developed by way of responses to his experiences carry in their wake the intention of liberating his body and soul. Teleologically speaking, salvation continues to be the moot point and existence in this world of mire never an end in itself. The duality lies in attempting to be an integral part of this world of pleasure symbolized by Chandri and the transcendental that is symbolized by religion. Chandri's truth is not the same as that of Praneshacharya, in fact they are antagonistic and there is, if we look into the 'utterances within utterances' of the woman, an unrelenting struggle between the two. The currents that the two unleash are at loggerheads, one is unified and the other is divided, and the intentions of their consciousness are governed by self-protection—and in the tussle it is Chandri who emerges as the stronger and cleverer one. She is the player par excellence in the games men and women play with each other.

Praneshacharya realizes after witnessing the cock-fight with Putta that "one part of lust is tenderness, the other part a demoniac will." Chandri too is not free from lust nor is she free from the urges to respectability. The sexual experience for Praneshacharya is so overpowering that it becomes a manifest dream in which there is a simultaneous production of past and present that fantasizes a future. The original experience of the cockfight releases subversive energies and becomes hallucinatory. In the violence there is an unconscious satisfaction and a fear because sexuality seeps in: "The oneness, the monism, of desire and fulfillment" has its attendant complications. In the cock-fight Praneshacharya sees the quintessence of his being flash before his eyes like the temple and ribbons of women as well as wings, beaks, talons and knives. When he looks into the eyes of the others he sees his own self in all its hues and a regressive revision of crucial sexual experiences takes place in a jiffy. "Who knows what those eyes will say? As soon as eye meets eye, who knows what shape the uninformed will take? Elongated dark eyes. A black snake braid coming down her shoulder, over her breast. The girl swaying at the end of the bamboo pole. Knives—wings—beaks, feathers. In the forest dark, the offering of full breasts. Belli's earth coloured breasts. An unblinking eye that'll see everything as if it is wide open. Behind him. The bird is paralyzed by the stare of the black serpent. Dread. He turned around. It was true." (123)

It is not Chandri that he fantasizes on but Belli. The ambivalent fascination for worldly pleasures is strong and it appeals to his potency as a male. It is the pull of sex, all that his own wife Bhagirathi lacked, that suspends his rational faculties. The uncanny frission of terror and excitement is the insoluble dilemma that he must enact or die. The erotogenic pleasures arise in the middle of prolonged death scenes, be it Naranappa or a bird. It is not just Chandri but 'Belli's earth-coloured breasts'; if there are thoughts of Bhagirathi "the altar of his sacrifice," there go the prospects of sleeping with Padamavati. And all this when a bird is out to destroy another bird with knives tied on its feet. In this violence is buried the instinctual libidinous aggression that the man is not aware of. The acrobat female also has her sexual appeal for Praneshacharya's unconscious and he notices her breasts and while he does this he finds her braid reminding him of a snake which according to Freud is symbolic of the male genital.

The whispered meanings generated by the protagonist in a state of neurosis point towards the unconscious quest for sexual adventurism. Thus, we can say that Praneshacharya's sexuality due to repression knows no bounds once it is given a free play. Such widespread obsession with sexuality gives Praneshacharya an 'oceanic feeling' that helps in bonding between the isolated self and the rest of the world that his recent misadventures have pulled him away from—recover from repression and celebrate human passion. Anantha Murthy is here trying to lay bare his protagonist's unconscious mind before us without the ego's defences against the prohibitive impulses. Praneshacharya's psychic life consists of symbiotic anxieties, if there is fear there is also a chance of physical gratification and quietening of the unruly senses. These fantasies provide Praneshacharya the opportunity to escape from the load of religious authority that always seems to weigh on his chest. The free play of Praneshacharya's imagination betrays that, for the time being, guilt and reparation work in tandem. He is sublimating himself and trying to masquerade as the macho master of his destiny, specially where women are concerned.

Throughout we find that the subalterns are subordinated by history and possess no organized position to make their ideas effective. Therefore, their marginalization in *Samskara* is in keeping with the historical biases against them. What Gramsci had to say about their lack of a collective identity is true for our purposes because the subalterns fail to rally behind Chandri or others whenever they are pitted against the Brahmins. The precondition for strength is their being unified or attaining a collective dominant position which the Brahmins would not allow. The fever of Brahminism loosened by Naranappa's death imposes itself on the subalterns and the 'temperature curves' of the high born lower only when they have castigated the subalterns with full throated ease. Naranappa's funeral causes a rupture between the past and the present, helps refigure their wisdom in the middle of plague. The dissent, embodied by the presence of the Muslims, with received thought becomes an attempt to question the tyranny of sacrosanct and arbitrary Brahmin thought. The lower caste or subalterns are treated like juveniles that require constant surveillance and attendance by the Brahmins. Chandri's initiative in Naranappa's cremation is important because it is an enabling step for other subalterns—it is revolutionary because it points towards contesting the Brahmins. One almost suspects if God was a Brahmin exploiter that he should have created religion in such a way. Even the discursive power of the text seems to work against them and abet in the incorporation of the subaltern in the Brahmin economy. The Brahmin and the subaltern communities are segregated but crossing of borders does take place between them and whenever it happens the subalterns are exploited. Attempts are made to absorb the subalterns within the Brahmin economy by reducing them to servitude and by grabbing their meagre possessions. One does not know whether it is a strength or weakness of the novel that nowhere in it takes place a discursive deconstruction of the Brahmins at the hands of the subalterns, they simply accept their fate. The subalterns never attack the Brahmins verbally or by use of force. The novel connives in the stereotypical subjectification of the women and subalterns, Chandri being an exception because her decision about the funeral symbolizes the subaltern's latent capacity for activist ingenuity. Their fragmented identities are taken advantage of by Hinduism's patriarchs against whom Chandri unwittingly plays the role of a subversive agency. On the whole the subalterns do not have any say in decision making and the fetishized Brahminism reigns under threat. The novel does not provide space enough to conceptualize any alternate form of sociality. Putta by harping on his father being a Brahmin tries to foist an alternate genealogy in terms of the Hindu logic and thinking. Therefore, within *Samskara* the subalterns appear as a broken people, partially because of their lack of any homogeneity, for there are categories and divisions among the subalterns also.

Praneshacharya having coffee with Putta and stuck to his company despite the urges to rid himself of the plebian shows that his longings for Chandri had changed him attitudinally. He had risen above untouchability, at least in private intercourse, and had started realizing that all men were basically the same. Prior to his involvement with Chandri he would not have allowed himself or Putta this privilege. It is not merely a change in his attitude towards the subalterns and lower castes but those of them who belonged to his own Brahmin community and had committed the sin of taking untouchable mistresses. Praneshacharya had looked down upon Naranappa and Mahabala for their violation of their *dharma*—for having entered into an unholy bond with women of low, uncertain birth. To begin with both Naranappa and Mahabala were honourable men till they fell from grace due to their preferences for women that were not of the pure Brahmin stock. Praneshacharya's realization that there was a very thin line between sin and morality, that there could be situations where the distinction between sin and virtue was indistinguishable, that we condemn much because we do not comprehend enough, that general principles formulated over a prolonged period of time by any dominant elite cannot be converted into hard and fast rules for social conduct, that mortals are subject to psycho-physiological dives that are capable of overpowering them, that sexual repression and deprivation can hit even the strongest among us, that socio-religious practices of a society limit the freedom of an individual, that choices one exercises in life are not necessarily governed by reason but by instincts, that often one makes sacrifices that one makes on the strength of one's character can be crippling in some significant way, that social norms are insensitive to the sentiments and feelings of the individual, that dilemmas in life are the result of the clash of the individual will against tradition, and that people could be made to suffer through sheer ignorance and lack of proper understanding on the part of others. Therefore, our *Saṃskaras* that are responsible for sustaining our inner most selves and in forming our identity can also become the source of our misery, lead to our destruction if unprecedented and unanticipated situations arise in the course of our lives. The novel is a tribute to an honest man who despite all his training and grounding in his *Samskaras* finds it impossible to follow their diktats.

Work Cited

Anantha Murthy, U.R., *Samskara: A Rite for Dead Man.* Trans. A.K. Ramanujan. New Delhi: Oxford University Press, 1999.

Samskara and Varnasamskara

BRATI BISWAS
DSC (Eve.) College, University of Delhi

Samskara, a Kannada novel by U.R. Anantha Murthy, was published in 1965, and an English translation, by A.K. Ramanujan followed in 1976. The novel depicted the degenerate ways of a group of Southern Brahmins living within an Agrahara; a Brahmin colony. Pranesha, a good Brahmin, is their spiritual head or Acharya. Praneshacharya's inability to solve the problem posed by the death of the heretic Naranappa lead to Pranesha's questioning of the Brahmin/Hindu tradition. After his sexual encounter with Chandri, Naranappa's lowcaste mistress, Praneshacharya embarks on a quest, in search of his true self. He seeks a self that is not rooted in caste consciousness. Caste is the very basis of traditional Hinduism. His existential quest for meaning, takes him into the 'demonic' world of the 'other'—the lower caste Chandri, Putta, and Padmavati. Devoid of his identity as the 'Crest-Jewel of Vedic learning,' Pranesha flounders on the brink of this demonic, unfamiliar world. He feels he needs to shed his Brahminhood altogether to be liberated, and yet he is afraid to 'fall into the tigerish world of cockfights.' (127) He retreats in fear of being sucked into this vortex and almost tamely begins his journey back to his agrahara. The novel ends on this open-ended note. The question regarding Pranesha's ability to shed his Brahminhood completely, remains unanswered. The initial critical reaction to the novel centred around the issue of its anti-Brahminism. The novel depicts an insider's view of Brahmin society. In writing *Samskara*, Anantha Murthy was coming to terms with his own Madhva Brahmin upbringing.

Samskara calls into question the meaning of Hindu India, and of the institutions that help to define it. Foremost among the institutions is caste, a hierarchical ranking of social classes based on how pure or impure each is. Four social classes (varnas) are traditionally recognized: the Brahmins (Priests), the Kshatriyas (warriors), the Vaishyas (merchants), and the Shudras (Labourers).

The Brahmin, as the highest in the social ranking, must at all times be ritually pure since he, as the spokesman for the community, intercedes with the Gods. The Shudra, on the other hand, the lowest of the four classes, performs most of the polluting tasks. Thus, labour among the social classes is divided on the basis of purity and impurity.

Caste governs social relationship and confers a sense of identity on the individual. Intercaste marriage is taboo as it leads to pollution. Sexual relations across caste boundaries are considered equally polluting as they lead to confusion of classes (VarnaSamskara). For this reason, a woman's sexual behavior is carefully guarded.

This traditional Brahminical view of the caste system was supported through the authority of the sacred literature, the Vedas. The Brahmins were the keepers of the sacred traditions and they performed the sacrificial rituals. This accorded them a preeminent position in Hindu society. They represented the caste system as an integrated and harmonious hierarchical structure, where even the Shudras docilely agreed to their debasement.

This was achieved through the religious doctrine of Karma, which stipulated that every act had an inevitable effect on the fate of the actors. A person's social rank, too, was determined by his karma in a previous life. There is no such thing as an accident of birth, for a person determines what he becomes by his action. A low-caste person, thinks he must expiate numerous 'sins' committed in past life, and that leading an exemplary life will earn him a better fate the next time around. The lower castes therefore have everything to gain by strict compliance with ritual demands. The Shudra's internalization of the Hindu order made them accept their abject social and economic position as legitimate. The untouchables were perceived as the indispensable complement to Brahmins. This was a stereotypical and idealized picture.

The non-Brahmin movements in Tamil Nadu and Maharashtra in the 20th century seriously contested the Brahminical notion of caste. These movements focused on the really degrading conditions of the lower castes and exposed the exploitative and repressive nature of the caste system. Though Gandhi too criticized untouchability, he supported the caste system and advocated Varnashrama dharma, that is, caste based division of labour. Ambedkar, on the other hand, viewed the caste system as the most vile and exploitative institution of Hinduism.

In modern India caste still remains an important marker of a person's identity. Tradition cannot be forgotten overnight, however desirable this may be. Caste is a fact of existence in secular India, and untouchability though illegal, has not entirely disappeared. Durvasapura is a microcosm of Brahmin India. The writing of the novel can be viewed as a *Samskara*—a rite of expiation, to atone for the oppressiveness of Brahminism. In *Samskara* the Brahmins and the untouchables form the two poles of the Hindu social order, representing the pure, and the impure. The notion of Dharma and Karma pervade the whole text. These concepts form the core of Pranesha's dilemma as he debates between action and non-action. These karmic notions at the heart of Hindu philosophy are negotiated from a purely Brahminical point of view. The fact that these Karmic notions of Brahminism were used as tools of repression and exploitation of the lower castes and the untouchables remains completely erased from the discourse of the text.

Samskara is a densely layered novel, depicting the individual journey of the central protagonist Pranesha, from the centre to the periphery and a return to that centre possibly with an altered vision about it. The women and the outcastes continue to remain on the periphery and his perceptions about them remain unaltered. Their condition does not affect him. The novel uses myth, symbol, allegory with realism to portray the complexities of the world it depicts. It is a world that is on the threshold of modernity but steeped in the traditional. The Brahmin agrahara is the microcosm of modern India where the role of the secular law books exist with traditionally sanctioned laws. The secular and religious laws chart contradictory courses.

This dichotomy is mockingly used by Naranappa. He flouted all Brahminical traditions and still continued to live in the Agrahara without fear of being excommunicated. He did all that was taboo for a Brahmin. He drove his Brahmin wife out of his house and started living with Chandri, an outcaste prostitute. He eats and drinks forbidden things like fish, meat and liquor. He throws the Saligrama, holy stone, sacred to Vishnu and worshipped by the Madhva Brahmins into the Tunga river and spits after it. He fishes from the holy temple pond with his Muslim friends and threatens to become a Muslim. The Brahmins cannot excommunicate him because had he become a Muslim, the Brahmins of Durvasapura would have had no option but to leave the Agrahara to escape pollution. "if he had really become a Muslim," observes Lakshmana, "no law could have thrown him out of the Brahmin Agrahara. We would have to leave" hence they endure his blasphemy in silence.

Lakshmana's speech is an acknowledgement of the power of the secular law over the religious in modern India. When it becomes impractical, the Brahmins disregard their religious laws. Being an upper caste male, Naranappa is able to successfully invoke the secular laws of the land for his protection, from his greedy, neighbours. The references to the Congress Party, the Army, and court litigation being fought by the agrahara Brahmins all reflect the Brahminical male's participation in the modern secular world outside.

The women, on the other hand, do not participate in this world. The upper caste woman's domain was to maintain the ritual purity of the Brahmins. The Brahmins enforce repressive control over the upper caste women's sexuality. The text represents them as sexually repressed and unattractive. This is used to legitimize the sexual transgressions of the Brahmin male.

The modern discourse of gender and caste equality does not find place within the mythic construction of these categories in the text. The heretic Naranappa is the most modern among the Brahmins living in the agrahara. When he dies, various myths regarding the union between a Brahmin Ascetic and a lower caste woman or celestial temptresses are cited by the Brahmins to condone Naranappa's sexual transgressions. The myth of Matsyagandhi, Sankara and Maneka are used to legitimize Brahmin male sexual transgression. The use of myth and legend to represent lower caste female sexuality reiterates the traditional stereotype of the easy and willing availability of these women for the sexual satisfaction of the Brahmin/upper caste male, and further reinscribes it in the modern age.

Chandri, Naranappa's mistress, occupies a space that is ambiguous. As a prostitute Chandri anyway falls outside the social order. Chandri epitomizes the position of the outcaste in Hindu Brahmin society. She lives within Naranappa's house, does all the wifely duties and yet is not a wife. She therefore has no legal/ritual right over his property or death rites. Her gender, caste and transgressive social position render her unfit. Ironically it is Chandri who inherits Naranappa's gold and cremates him.

Chandri cremates Naranappa with the help of a Muslim. She decides to do so out of sheer practical necessity and not out of any desire to question Brahminism. Though her action could be represented as a radical flouting of Brahminical traditions, the text does not do so. The untouchable is represented as having internalized the codes of Hinduism, and thus she is shown as respecting the codes and accepting her exploitation meekly. She readily becomes the facilitator/mediator of Pranesacharya's rite of passage from an Ascetic to the man of the world. She accepts his sexual overtures as a blessing. The novel represents the conflict between Praneshacharya and Naranappa as the conflict between the Vedantic and the Materialist schools of thought. Another binary that exists between the Brahmin and the lower castes is not elaborated. But, the radical potential of the lower caste point of view, to offer a counter discourse to Brahminism, is glossed over. The end of the novel remains flawed in terms of a satisfactory conclusion. Its inconclusiveness reflects the difficulty of resolving the caste issue satisfactorily.

In his attempt to highlight Brahmin degeneracy, Anantha Murthy imbues the lower caste Chandri, with a positive and regenerative potential. Chandri is represented as selfless, giving and caring. She is like Mother Nature and is compared to the Tunga river which washes away all sins. She is a life-giver, she mediates between the world of Praneshacharya and Naranappa. She initiates Praneshacharya into the material world of physical and sensual pleasures. She acts as the catalyst for his initiation into the real world of men. She symbolizes the positive life giving force of Nature. Her fertility and fecundity is emphasized through her desire for a child by Praneshacharya the Holy Man; the modern day parallel to the Sages of ancient times. Throughout the novel, the allegorical and the real co-exist. Thus, it would be wrong to see Chandri as only an allegorical, symbolic, mythic being. She is a real woman and reveals real feelings and desires. Most critics highlight her symbolic, aesthetic and allegorical significance in the text and gloss over her real status vis-a-vis the Brahmin society. This is probably because Anantha Murthy has represented her mainly in this manner, and she does not represent herself. Most of the time she is represented and figured through the lusting gaze of the Brahmin men of the agrahara. She is the 'object' of their collective fantasy and desire. Except Praneshacharya, all the other men in the agrahara envy Naranappa's luck in having her as his mistress.

Significantly when Chandri does represent herself, her self-delineation is through her mother. Being the daughter of a prostitute she does not know who her father is. She is the transgressing female, an outcaste. As a prostitute she remains outside society and its rigid moral code. Social norms defining codes for wives, and widows do not apply to her. Yet she desires a child by Praneshacharya. Though a very natural instinct, it also reflects her internalization of Hindu concepts regarding prostitutes. "Chandri was afraid that Praneshacharya might scold her, despise her. There was also a hope in her that his touch might bear fruit in her body. And a gratefulness that she too might have earned merit." (65) Matsyagandhi is the scriptural representation of the lower caste woman in the text. Chandri hopes to be as blessed as Matsyagandhi was in the myth. The lower caste woman believes that she can hope to attain salvation by serving and satiating the sexual passion of the Godlike Brahmin Ascetic. This was the argument behind the Devadasi system which exploited the sexuality of lower caste women in the name of service to God. These women were in fact sexually exploited by the priestly Brahmins.

The Varna/caste system ascribes particular characteristics to the different castes. The Brahmin was satvik (pure) and Shudra was Tamasik (lazy). Traditional representation of the Shudra was in these terms. Anantha Murthy avoids such stereotyping. He attempts a sympathetic representation of the lower castes. Though sympathetic, it still remains a Brahmin view of the lower castes.

The text fails to give representation to lower caste perceptions of the caste system which was radically different from the Brahmin view of consensus and harmony. Though there is consensus and internalization of the caste system by the untouchables, they also represent themselves differently. They are both part of society and yet separate. The caste system exempts the lower castes from certain purificatory rites or *Samskaras*. This exemption made them less ritualistic and more practical. Chandri's disposal of Naranappa's corpse is an instance of such practical wisdom. But it is not adequately highlighted as representing a positive alternative and counter discourse to Brahminic philosophy.

If the Brahmin life is all about Dharma, then the Shudra life revolves around Karma or action. While the Brahmin maintains his Dharma, the Shudra attends to his karma of doing menial but practical jobs to preserve the Brahminical purity. The Brahmins made a virtue out of non-action. And Praneshacharya's fear of action stems from having internalized this concept.

The novel, set in the colonial era, just before India was to achieve its freedom from British rule does not reflect the emancipatory tendencies of a resurgent India. Though a critique of Brahminism was very much part of the social and political climate of the times, the lower caste characters in the novel do not seem to be aware of it. Naranappa, the modern Brahmin taunts Praneshacharya - "Your texts and rites don't work anymore. The Congress Party is coming to power; you'll have to open up the temples to all outcastes." (20) The critique of traditional Brahminism and the caste system emerged from, both the West and from within Indian society. The colonial strategy to discredit Brahminism began, post the 1857 Mutiny. The Mutiny was largely fed by the Brahmins, and this made the British recruit the lower castes into the army (Natarajan 167). This allowed the lower castes an option out of their traditionally inferior jobs within Hindu society. Thus, the perception about the colonial rule among the lower castes and the Brahmins vastly differed. For instance, the agrahara Brahmins view the Army as a polluting influence whereas many lower caste activists hailed the colonial enterprise as emancipatory for themselves. This reflects that there is no one given 'tradition' at any one given time. Traditions are ultimately ideological constructions liable to change according to changing times and people.

Thus, there exist various 'traditions' within Hindu philosophy. In the novel, Praneshacharya represents the Spiritualist school, while Naranappa represents the Materialist school. The other Brahmins in the agrahara and elsewhere are divided according to different sects they belong to. The Madhvas and the Smartas are the two predominant sects. The novel realistically depicts their differences. Though the ideal of a unified sense of Brahminism remains elusive, the question of what constitutes Brahminism acts as a unifying principle of the narrative. Praneshacharya's agonizing over his loss of Brahminhood reiterates this question at various levels of the text. Praneshacharya's inability to resolve the problem and arrive at any satisfactory resolution suggests that ultimately such a quest is flawed and doomed to failure. By the end of the novel, Praneshacharya begins to comprehend the differences and interconnectedness between all things. But he is unable to surrender his Brahminhood and accept the un-Brahminical world-view. His inability to accept the un-Brahminical as a viable alternative, limits him. Would he learn to combine the two world-views, remains an open-ended question like the ending of the novel.

NOTES

Anantha Murthy, U.R. *Samskara*, trans. A.K. Ramanujan (Delhi: OUP, 1976).

_____, "The Search for an Identity: A Kannada Writer's Viewpoint," *Vagartha*: 15 (October 1976), pp. 1-15.

Deliege, Robert, *The Untouchables of India*, trans. Nora Scott (U.K.: berg Publishers, 1999).

Mukherjee, Meenakshi '*Samskara*,' *Realism and Reality: The Novel and Society in India* (New Delhi: OUP, 1988).

Natarajan, Nalini. "Gender and Caste: Modernity in U.R. Anantha Murthy's *Samskara*," *U.R. Anatha Murthy's "Samskara": A Critical Reader*, ed. K.C. Baral, et al (Delhi: Pencraft International, 2005).

Samskara: A Rite for a Dead Man: Concept of *Karma* and Theory of *Gunas*: An Interpretation

SHRAWAN K. SHARMA
Gurukul Kangri University, Haridwar

> The present ambiguity, this Trishanku-state. I'll be free from it only through a free deliberate wide-awake fully-willed act. Otherwise a piece of string in the wind, a cloud taking on shapes according to the wind. I have become a mere thing. (109-10)

U.R. Anantha Murthy's *Samskara: A Rite for a Dead Man* is one of the masterpieces of Asian literature. It is, in fact, as inconceivable to talk about Praneshacharya, the Crest-Jewel of the Vedanta Philosophy without his soliloquies and interior monologues as to talk about the novel *Samskara: A Rite for a Dead Man* without Praneshacharya. There are at least as many ways of looking at the Acharya of the agrahara from the point of view of his encounters with different characters as the opinions expressed by his literary critics. Praneshacharya is constantly seen lost in his soliloquies and interior monologues which unfold his transformation from a fully evolved socialized Brahmin at one with his tradition towards a new kind of person. A careful perusal of Praneshacharya's soliloquies and interior monologues show that he can be conceived in terms of Air, Poet, Mind, Introvert, Spiritual, Jewel rather than Earth, Peasant, Heart, Animal, Extrovert and Metal. The qualities of the Acharya are associated with the '*sâttavik guna.*' The present approach to the Acharya takes into consideration two aspects, the concept of '*karma*' and the theory of '*gunâs.*' The present attempt aims at realizing Praneshacharya's ideal of disinterested action and attaining the level of '*gunâtita*'

The starting point to discuss the Acharya is his disgust with his social self. When the Brahmins come in a herd to him for his guidance, he thinks, looks around and questions himself: "What manner of man am I? I am just like you—a soul driven by lust and hate. Is this my first lesson in humility? Come, Chandri, tell them, relieve me of Guru's burden." He says to the Brahmins: "I'm lost. I couldn't get Maruti to say anything. I know nothing. You do whatever your hearts say."[1]

From this realization comes the introspection of his own inner nature in his monologues and leads to self-enquiry and a longing for liberation which in Sanskrit is called '*mumuksutva.*' His turning away from all worldly activity, '*vyavhâra,*' is the source of his so called inaction. The fact that the Acharya contrasts himself with Mahabala, Naranappa and Puttu is of special significance. His questionings indicate his notion about the nature of decision. There are two attitudes to life in Indian philosophical thinking, one is '*pravrtti mârga*' which means indulging in all kinds of action and the other is the '*nivrtti mârga*' which means turning away from all external action. While the former engages himself in what Wordsworth would mean by "The world is too much with us, getting and spending," the latter turns inward and engages himself in self-analysis and self-enquiry in an introvert fashion. Obviously, Praneshacharya belongs to the latter type and his monologues give an insight into his introvert personality.

II

Action is indicated by the word '*karma*' in Sanskrit. '*Karma*' not only means action but the result of the action thereof. There are three types of '*karmas*' in Indian philosophical thinking

i) *Sanchit karma*, the result of the past action which has collected itself,

ii) '*Prârabdha karma,*' that part of the '*sanchit karma*' which has started bearing fruit at present,

iii) '*Agâmi karma,*' that part of '*sanchit karma*' which is still to bear fruit in the future.

As far as the discussion of the Acharya is concerned, we are dealing with the second category namely '*prârabdh karma.*' There are other types of '*karmâs*' also:

i) '*Kâmya karma,*' action performed with a desire to get something in return

ii) '*Nisiddha karma,*' forbidden action

iii) '*Prâyashchit karma,*' expiatory action

iv) '*Nishakama karma,*' performance of actions disinterestedly—without attachment to the fruit of the action thereof—the one that is recommended in the *Gitâ:* '*karmanyevâdhikaraste maphaleshukadâchana*'[2]

Indeed, what is termed fatal law in the Acharya is that he thinks ceaselessly for achieving a state, called '*nishakâm karma siddhi*' after his encounter with Chandri in the fashion of the great sages—Parashara who impregnated Matsyagandha in the boat and fathered Vyasa, Vishwamitra who lost all the merits of penance for Menaka—and wonders how they faced such experiences. "Could they have lived, seeing life itself as renunciation, staying with God, going beyond conflicts and opposites by living through them, taking on every changing shape that earth craves and offers, flowing finally into formlessness in the ocean like a river." The monologue impels to believe that "salvation is possible through intoxication as by self discipline, through violation as through observance of Law." (144) Hence he surrenders everything to God, saying:

> if I don't tell the agrahara Brahmins, if Naranappa's body is not cremated, I cannot escape fear. If I decide to live with Chandri without telling any one, the decision is not complete, not fearless. I must come now to a final decision. All things indirect must become direct. Must pierce straight in the eye. But it is agony either way. If I hide things, all through life I will be agonized by the fear

> of discovery, by some onlooking eye. If I don't, I will muddy the life of others by opening up and exposing truth to the every eye my brahminhood has lived and grown by. O God, take from me the burden of decision. Just as it happened in the dark of the jungle, without my will, may this decision too happen. May it happen all at once. May a new life come into being before I blink my eye. (132)

Evidently it is seen that the Acharya achieves the state of '*nishakâma karma*,' performance of actions disinterestedly—without attachment to the fruit of the action thereof. Now he has "no taint of repentance," "no trace of sorrow,"

III

This is a quintessential passage to place the Acharya in the philosophical framework as it describes the qualities of a '*gunâtita*' or '*sthitiprajna*.' However before this, the definition of the *gunas* themselves has to be taken note of:

> sattvam rajas tama iti
> gunah prakrtisambhavah
> nibandhnanti mahabaho
> dehedehinamavvayam
>
> tatra sattvam nirmalatvat
> prakasakam anamayam
> sukhasangena badhnati
> jnanasangenaca nagha
>
> rajoragatmakam viddhi
> trsnasangasamudbhavam
> tan nibadhnatikaunteya
> karmasangena dehinam
>
> tama tv ajnanajam viddhi
> mohanam sarvadehinam
> paramdalsyanidrabhis
> tan nibadhnatibharata[2]

The three modes ('*gunâs)* goodness *('sattva*'), passion ('*rajas*'), and dullness ('*tamas*') born of nature ('*prakrti*') bind down in the body. O mighty armed, Arjuna, the imperishable dweller in the body.

Of these, goodness ('*sattva*') being pure, causes illumination and health. It binds, O blameless one, by attachment to happiness and by attachment to knowledge.

Passion ('*rajas*') know then, is of the nature of attraction, springing from craving and attachment. It binds fast, O sun of Kunti, the embodied one by attachment to action.

But dullness ('*tamas*') know thou is born of ignorance and deludes all embodied beings. It binds, O Bharata, by developing the qualities of negligence, indolence and sleep.

This contemplation of the three '*gunâs*' leads us directly to the theory of '*gunâs*' as defined in the *Gitâ:*

prakasam ca pravrttim ca
moham eva ca pandava
na dvestisampravrttani
na nivtttaani kanaksati

udasinavad asino
gunair yo na vicalyate
guna vartanta ity eva
yo 'vatisthatine' ngate
samadukhasukhah svasthah
samalostasmakanchanah
tulyapriyaiyodhiras
tulyanindatmasamstutih

manapamanayostulyas
tulyo mitraripaksayoh
sarvarmbhaparityagi
gunatitah sa ucyate[3]

He, O Pandava, who does not abhor illumination, activity and delusion when they arise nor longs for them when they cease.

He who is seated like one unconcerned, unperturbed by the modes who stands apart, without wavering, knowing that is only the mode that acts.

> He who regards pain and pleasure alike, who dwells in his own Self, who looks upon a clod, a stone, a piece of gold as of equal worth, who remains the same amidst the pleasant and the unpleasant things, who is firm of mind, who regards both blame and praise as one.
>
> He who is the same in honour and dishonour and same to the friends and foes and who has given up all initiative of action, he is said to have risen above the modes

In the verses quoted above the words, 'it is only the modes that act' and 'who has given up all initiative of action,' are of special significance in determining the meaning of action and inaction. To raise above the modes is the ideal towards which Praneshacharya is working. In him '*sattvaguna*' is predominant. A '*sattvika*' is described by Radhakrishnan in the following way:

> The three modes are present in all human beings, though in different degrees. No one is free from them and in each soul one or the other predominates. Men are said to be '*sattvika*,' '*rajasa*' and '*tamasa*' according to the mode which prevails. When the theory of the humours of the body determined physiology, men were divided into the sanguine, the bilious, the lymphatic and the nervous according to the predominance of one or the other of the four humours. In the Hindu classification, the psychic characteristics are taken into account. The '*sâttvika*' nature aims at light and knowledge, the '*rajasa*' nature always wishes to be active and cannot sit still and its activities are limited by selfish desires, the '*tamas*' nature is dull and inert; its mind is dark and confused and its whole life is one continuous submission to environment.
>
> '*Sattva*' does not get rid of the ego-sense. It also causes desire though for noble objects. The self which is free from all attachment is here attached to happiness and knowledge. Unless we cease to think and will with the ego-sense, we are not liberated.[4]

The fact that the struggle that we see in Praneshacharya is the struggle of a '*sadhaka*' and through '*sâdhana*' he wants to rise above being a mere '*sâttvika*' to the final level of '*gunâtita.*' To put in Radhakrishnan's words, "Even '*sâttvika*' goodness is imperfect since this goodness has for its condition the struggle with its opposite. The moment the struggle ceases and the goodness becomes absolute, it ceases to be goodness and goes beyond all ethical compulsion. By developing the nature of '*sattva*,' we rise beyond it and obtain transcendental wisdom. Just as we pull out a thorn by a thorn, so renouncing worldly things we must renounce renunciation *(kantakam kantakeneva yena tyajasi tam tyaja)*. By means of '*sattva*' we overcome '*rajas*' and '*tamas*' and then get beyond '*sattva*' itself. This is precisely Praneshacharya's ideal towards which he is relentlessly moving. His struggle ceases to be mere goodness. He believes that only a man of "Goodness" can reach salvation. He now wants to go beyond thinking and beyond all ethical compulsion. There is all the difference between a '*sâttvika*' that Praneshacharya is and the '*gunâtita*' that he is trying to be. Praneshacharya's '*sattvaguna*' manifests itself in his luminosity and his essential nobility and greatness. His life is full of religious faith, full of scriptural wisdom and full of moral discipline and integrity. The Acharya had long before decided to renounce the world; he had decided to become a '*sanyâsi*'; he had decided to live a life of self-sacrifice.

That was the ideal, the challenge, of his boyhood days. So he had married a born invalid deliberately. He had left her in the grateful house of her father, gone to Benares, studied to become 'the Crest-Jewel of Vedanta Philosophy' and had come back. . . . He had cooked for her, fed her the wheat gruel he had himself made, done meticulously every act of daily worship for the gods, read and explicated the holy texts for the Brahmins—the *Ramayana*, the *Mahabharata*, the *Bhagavata*, etc.—hoarded his penances like a miser his money. A hundred thousand mantras chanted and counted this month, another hundred thousand the next, a couple of hundred thousand for the eleventh day of the moon. Million by million, he counted his earnings, penances reckoned on the beads of his Basil-rosary. (76)

Here it would be worthwhile to take into account the opening narration about Praneshacharya and his born invalid wife, Bhagirathi, which enables the reader to look into the noble life of the Acharya for the last twenty years and gathers a lot of respect for him. Such a life of the Acharya witnesses a rare combination of moral qualities in him:

> He [Acharya] bathed Bhagirathi's body, a dried up pea-pod and wrapped a fresh sari around it; then he offered food and flowers to the Gods as he did everyday, put the flowers in her hair and gave her holy water. She touched his feet, he blessed her. Then he brought her a bowlful of cracked-wheat porridge from the kitchen.
>
> Bhagirathi said in a low voice, 'You finish your meal first.'
>
> 'No, no. Finish your porridge. That first.'
>
> The words were part of a twenty-year old routine between them. A routine that began with the bath at dawn, twilight prayers, cooking, medicines for his wife. And crossing the stream again to the Maruti temple for worship. That was the daily unfailing routine. After their meals, the Brahmins of agrahara would come to the front of his house, one by one, and gather there to listen to his recitation of sacred legends, always new and always dear to them and to him. In the evening he would take another bath, say more twilight prayers, make porridge for his wife, cook, eat dinner. Then there would be more recitations for the brahmins who gathered again on the verandah.
>
> Now and then Bhagirathi would say: 'Being married to me is no joy. A house needs a child. Why don't you just get married again? Praneshacharya laughed aloud. 'A wedding for an old man.'
>
> 'Come now, what kind of an old man are you? You haven't touched forty yet. Any father would love to give you his girl and bless her with wedding water. You studied Sanskrit in Kashi. . . . A house needs a child to make it home. You have had no joy in this marriage.'
>
> Praneshacharya would not answer. He would smile and pat his wife. . . . Didn't Lord Krishna say: Do what is to done with no thought of fruit? The Lord definitely means to test him on his way to salvation; that is why, he has given him a Brahmin birth this time and set him up in this kind of family. The Acharya is filled with pleasure and a sense of worth as sweet as the five-fold nectar of holy days; he is filled with compassion for his ailing wife. He proudly swells a little at his lot thinking, 'by marrying an invalid, I get ripe and ready.' (1-2)

He held: "I am born with such one 'Good' nature. This invalid wife is the sacrificial altar for my sacrifices." (76) It was the same acharya in whom the Brahmins of agrahara had an unfathomable faith. They hold:

> He knows all alliances and misalliances, has studied it all in Kashi, he knows all the scriptures, earned the title Crest-Jewel of Vedic Learning. . . . Our Acharya has won all sorts of arguments with all super pundits, yours and ours, won honours at every seat of learning in the south, fifteen lace shawls and silver platters. (6)

Even Naranappa, the Acharya's opposite in number, considered him to be a real Brahmin for the simple reason of his intellect, wisdom and conduct unlike that of other brahmins of the agrahara. He once said to him: "I'll destroy Brahminism, I certainly will. My only sorrow is that there is no brahminism really left to destroy in this place—except you." (23)

In order to analyze the character of the Acharya, let us understand the '*gunas*' in terms of '*koúas*' (organs of action or sheath) which are described in Indian philosophy. The koshas are five in number—the '*annamâya*' (the sheath of gross food), '*pranamaya*' (the sheath of Vital Airs), '*manomâya*' (the sheath of the Mind), the '*vijnyanamâya*' (the intelligent sheath of Consciousness) and the '*ânandamaya*' (the sheath of Bliss). As '*sattvaguna*' has an excess of luminosity, it is associated with the vijnanamayakosha (the sheath of Consciousness). Praneshacharya, the intellectual, is to be associated with the consciousness of '*kartritva*' and '*bhokritva*' (an agent and enjoyer) that is happy or enjoyer etc. He is a '*mumukshu*' (one who strives for liberation) and wants to become a '*gunâtiti*' (one who rises above the three *gunâs*). This process naturally takes for granted that he becomes '*dwanwatita*' (above the apparent binary contractions). He is entangled in the overwhelming question of how to get over '*kartritva*' or giving up all initiatives for action and being able to regard pain and pleasure, honour and insult alike. He, dwelling in one's own self, prepares himself to embrace the truth and thus overcomes all conflict and dualities. His last monologue is indicative of this state:

> I'll reach the agrahara by midnight, far away from this world. In full view of the frightened Brahmins, I'll stand exposed like the naked quick of life; and I, elder in their midst, will turn into a new man at midnight. . . . When I'll tell them about myself, there should be no taint of repentance in me, no trace of any sorrow that I am a sinner. (135)

This is the admirable quality in Praneshacharya—the quality of '*titiksha*'—the overcoming of conflict and dualities. Praneshacharya has '*samâdhanam*' of a certain kind (the constant concentration of the mind) as a result of his '*uparati*' (cessation of a certain type of external action which has given him the '*virâga*' (turning away of worldly ambition) and achieving '*vairâgya*' (philosophical disinterestedness in worldly affairs). Praneshacharya holds in one of his monologues already quoted before: "O God, take from me the burden of decision. Just as it happened in the dark of the jungle, without my will, may this decision too happen. May it happen all at once. May a new life come into being before I blink my eye." (132)

NOTES

U.R. Anantha Murthy, *Samskara: A Rite for a Dead Man*, trans. A.K. Ramanujan (New Delhi: Oxford University Press, 1978), p. 77.

The Bhagavadagita, ed. Radhakrishnan with an introductory essay (London: George Allen and Unwin, 1948) Chapter XIV, Verses 5-8, 22-25.

Desecration of Religious Values in Graham Greene's *The Power and the Glory* and Anantha Murthy's *Samskara*: A Comparative Study

BASAVARAJ NAIKAR
Karnatak University, Dharwad

That the aim of comparative study of literatures is to show the essential unity of human life is borne out by the present study of Graham Greene's *The Power and the Glory* and U.R. Anantha Murthy's *Samskara*. Though both the texts depict two different religious contexts, yet one may see a few striking similarities between the two which help us to understand the common human tendencies all over the world.

Graham Greene's *The Power and the Glory* delineates the life of a priest against the atheistic background to Mexico whereas Anantha Murthy's *Samskara* depicts the life of a brahmin priest against an orthodox religious background. But the common theme in both the novels happens to be the desecration of religious values. As the only priest surviving in the anti-clerical Mexico, the anonymous priest is expected to uphold the high ideals of Roman Catholicism. Similarly Praneshacharya, the head-priest of Durvasapura who was educated at Kashi and has earned the title, "the Crest-Jewel of Vedanta Philosophy" is expected to uphold the ideals of Madhva brahminism. It is on account of the moral responsibility, that those protagonists are respected by the believers of their respective faiths. The priest, though hunted by the lieutenant, representative of the Mexican Government, is looked up to by the people who are still in need of religion. Likewise Praneshacharya is respected by the brahmins of Durvasapura as a moral referee.

But the protagonists have, unfortunately, not been able to live upto the ideals expected of them. Both of them have desecrated their holy ideals, because of their weaknesses of flesh. The priest of *The Power and the Glory* has committed not only venial sins like lying, drinking, but also mortal sins like fornication. Because of his morbid alcoholism he has been nicknamed as a 'whisky priest' showing the in-built contradiction. He has committed fornication with Maria in a moment of drunken loneliness and begotten an illegal child called Brigitta. He is aware of his sins and feels contrition. He is even mocked by his own' beloved Maria as follows:

> I know you're a bad priest. That time we were together I bet that wasn't all you've done. I've heard things, I can tell you. Do you think God wants you to stay and die--a whisky priest like you? . . . Suppose you die. You'll be a martyr, won't you? What kind of a martyr do you think you'll be? It's enough to make people mock. (*PG*, 79)

Similarly Praneshacharya who hates Naranappa for having desecrated the brahminical values in his life, cannot decide now whether proper brahminical death-rite should be rendered to the dead Naranappa. Praneshacharya not only fails to take any decision about Naranappa's death-rite but even degenerates into Naranappa's anti-brahminical sinfulness. Naranappa who ate fish and flesh, drank liquor and slept with the lowcaste Chandri had been notorious for his anti-brahminical behaviour. But, paradoxically enough, Praneshacharya also, in spite of being the Crest-Jewel of Vedanta Philosophy, stoops to the level of having sexual intercourse with Chandri. There is thus no essential difference between Naranappa and Praneshacharya as the latter's dubious asceticism is suddenly transformed into irresistible eroticism. Hence his high idealism of brahminism is thrown to winds. Praneshacharya enjoys the recollection of his adulterous experience with Chandri and her seductive breasts, buttocks and thighs. Adultery or fornication, thus, happens to be the common denominator of their degeneration, though the cultural contexts leading them to the sin are different. Whereas the whisky priest was compelled to indulge in fornication with Maria by his drunkenness and loneliness, Praneshacharya is tempted to have his sexual fulfillment with the lowcaste Chandri when he is fully conscious of himself. The superficial brahminical or Vedantic discipline is shattered when the floodgates of his suppressed sexual desire are opened at the slightest stimulation by Chandri in the forest at night. After having sex with Chandri, he begins to rationalize his action and even draw inspiration from Naranappa's libidinous life, Mahabala's living with a prostitute at Kashi and Shripati's regular fornication with the lowcaste Belli. He even feels tempted to visit the prostitute Padmavati at the Fair. Praneshacharya, thus, becomes a symbol of sudden degeneration of brahminical asceticism and triumph of elemental sexual instinct, or of Lawrentian dark-gods.

A difference between the whisky priest and Praneshacharya which could be noted is that whereas the fornication with Maria remains in the former as a desiccated memory, that with Chandri remains in the latter as a very lush and exciting memory.

Both the protagonists of the novels have committed any venial or minor sins in addition to the moral or grand *(Maha papa)* sin of fornication. Whereas the whisky priest is addicted to alcoholism and gets insulted, mocked at and imprisoned for that reason, Praneshacharya commits a similar, if not the same, crime, in the brahminical context. After losing his invalid wife Praneshacharya is in a mourning period. Unable to decide about the yes or no of Naranappa's funeral, but yet under the intoxicating memory of his fornication with Chandri, Praneshacharya leaves his native village for Dharmasthala Monastery where he partakes of the community meal. Though he knows that it is wrong to desecrate the Monastery by eating the meal there when he is still mourning the death of his wife, he does so only because of his inability to control his hunger. He wants to rationalize this desecration as an emergency-ethic *(apad-dharma)*. In both the cases i.e. of the whisky priest and Praneshacharya, the desires of body triumph over those of spirit thereby showing their fall from the spiritual height.

Lying is a venial or minor sin committed by both the protagonists. The whisky priest is guilty of this sin when he tells the lieutenant that his name is Monrez and the half-caste that he is not a reverend father but only a genetic father. He has this recourse to lying in order to hide his identity and escape from dangerous or embarrassing situations. Similarly Praneshacharya lies to the other brahmins of his own as well as other agraharas and to Putta in order to escape their inquisitive notice.

Both the protagonists undergo an experience of metaphorical hell as a sort of punishment for their sinful behaviour. The whisky priest has a vision of hell in the prison cell where he is confined. The acrid smell of urinals and lavatory buckets, the drone of mosquitoes, shameless sexuality, criminality, agnosticism and physical discomfiture add to the whisky priest's vision of objective hell, though, of course, he feels quite comfortable in the company of other criminals. Similarly Praneshacharya also undergoes an experience of the demonic world introduced to him by Putta when the latter takes the former through the temple-festival and fair, whorehouse and pawnshop. The demonic world is full of passion and sensation like cock fighting, eating, drinking, and whoring etc. But unlike the priest who feels comfortable in the company of sinners in the dark cell, Praneshacharya does not feel totally at ease in the demonic world though he is slowly hardened enough to bear with it. Thus both the whisky priest and Praneshacharya have a temporary experience of descent into (unchristian and unbrahminical) hell.

In both the novels, the protagonists are attacked by their opponents for their degeneration and fall from the height of ideals. The lieutenant who represents the materialistic point of view of the Mexican Government ideologically attacks the whisky priest for making a farce of the religious institution.

> "The other," the lieutenant said, "is a priest," He raised his voice: "You know what this means--traitor to the republic. Anyone who shelters him is a traitor too?" Their immobility seemed to anger him. He said, "You're fools if you still believe what the priests tell you. All they want is your money. What has God ever done for you? Have you got enough to eat? Have your children got enough

> to eat? Instead of food they talk to you about heaven. Oh, everything will be fine after you are dead, they say. I tell you—everything will be fine when *they* are dead, and you must help." (*PG*, 74)

It is because of the hypocrisy of the religious people that the materialistic or communistic Government of Mexico is bent upon abolishing all religion and killing all the priests in the State.

Likewise Praneshacharya and his dubious brahminism are also ideologically attacked by the inimical groups of people, especially Naranappa who stands for anti-brahminical values of life.

"O Acharya, who in the world can live with a girl who gives no pleasure—except of course some barren brahmins!" "You fellows-your brahmins—you want to tie me to a hysterical female, just because she is some relative, right? Just keep your dharma to yourself--we've but one life—I belong to the "Hedonist School"—which says—Borrow, borrow, if you must, but drink your ghee."

> The Acharya pleaded, "Do whatever you want to do yourself. Please don't corrupt these boys." He just laughed. "Your Garuda, he robs shaven widows, he plots evil with black magic men, and he is one of your brahmins, isn't he? . . . All right, let's see who wins,, Acharya. You or me? Let's see how long all this brahmin business will last. All your brahmin respectability. I'll roll it up and throw it all ways for a little bit of pleasure with one female. (*S*, 21)

\Thus in both the novels there is an ideological conflict between the religious protagonists and the irreligious antagonist. Unfortunately the protagonists are not able to live up to their own ideals because of their human weaknesses, thereby rightly deserving the contempt of their enemies. In fact, they are awakened to their sins and have some kind of repentance after making a thorough search of their souls. The self-examination makes them aware of their unworthiness. The whisky priest, for example, confesses before the lieutenant in a self-analytical way:

> That other priest was right. It was when he left I began to go to pieces. One thing went after another. I got careless about my du-

> ties. I began to drink. It would have been much better, I think, if I had gone, too. Because pride was at work all the time. Not love of God. . . . Pride was what made the angels fall. Pride's the worst thing for all. I thought I was a fine fellow to have stayed when the others had gone. And then I thought I was so grand I could make my own rules. I gave up fasting, daily Mass. I neglected my prayers—and one day because I was drunk and lonely—well, you know how it was, I got a child. (*PG*, 196)

Like the whisky priest, Praneshacharya also is aware of his weaknesses and tries to analyze his conduct retrospectively:

> I must examine unafraid even my belief that the moment occurred suddenly by itself, without my stir, in the darkness of the forest. It's true it occurred suddenly, I didn't go after it and get it. The outstretched hands touched the breasts—desire was born—there—there's the secret. That was the movement that decided which way to turn. The answer is not that my body accepted it, but in the darkness my hands fumbled urgently, searched for Chandri's things and buttocks as I had never searched dharma. In that moment, decisive of which way I should turn, I took the decision to take Chandri. Even if I lost control, the responsibility to decide was still mine. (98)

Thus both the whisky priest and Praneshacharya have an awareness of their sins or transgressions and take the responsibility upon them. But both of them cannot change their past or even the future and are in a way ready to accept the consequences of their action. Both of them feel a mental restlessness and undergo a psychological hell, which is almost parallel to their experience of objective hell (in the prison cell), or the demonic world (in the Festival and Fair).

A comparative study of the behaviour of the whisky priest and Praneshacharya, thus, reveals the common factor of their degeneration or fall from the height of ideals. The whisky priest has not been able to live up to the ideals of a Catholic saint. Similarly Praneshacharya has fallen from the brahminical height into an anti-brahminical level. The fall or degeneration of the two protagonists has, obviously, been caused by the weakness of flesh. Up this point, both of them are equal. But a further study of their behaviour shows that both of them are not equal, as one steals a march over the other. Comparatively speaking, the whisky priest appears to be far better than Praneshacharya because the former, in spite of being a degenerate figure, serves the purpose of his Catholic religion. In spite of being the weakest vessel, he becomes an instrument of God's cosmic design. As he confesses, "But it doesn't matter so much my being a coward—and all the rest. I can put God into a man's mouth just the same—and I can give him God's pardon. It wouldn't make any difference to that if every priest in the church was like me." (*PG*, 195) Though the whisky priest cannot rise to the level of a saint, yet he can perform the minimum duties of an ordinary priest and popularize or maintain the Catholic faith among the believers. God's love for mankind is so appalling and His glory so great that He can use even the weakest priest for the fulfillment of his providential purpose. All this makes clear that Graham Greene has an affirmative vision of life, which recognizes the overall teleological beauty of the universe in spite of the occasional ugliness, which shows that even the weakest person can become an instrument of God. In Graham Greene's world, the whisky priest, in spite of his so-called fall or degeneration, can keep the institution of religion going, and in spite of his personal damnation, can help the other believers have their salvation. He, thus, serves a positive role and becomes an embodiment of the novelist's affirmative vision of life.

But Anantha Murthy's vision of life depicted in *Samskara* appears to be negative and decadent. The novelist is just contented to show the degeneration of a brahmin from the dubious height of his ideals. Whereas Graham Greene shows the whisky priest struggling with an agnostic atmosphere for the continuation of religious ideals and solutions, Anantha Murthy shows a brahmin acharya coming from a religious atmosphere and yet becoming irreligious. Though the brahmin community, especially the Madhva sect, has put their trust in him as a moral referee, he does not live up to their expectations by subordinating his individual physical desires to the rational control and social responsibility. By his individual fall, he brings moral disaster to the entire community, which has put an extraordinary trust in him as the Crest-Jewel of Vedanta Philosophy. Instead of solving the problem of Naranappa's death-rite for the community, he stoops to sleep with the lowcaste Chandri and escapes from his village Durvasapura. He has no desire to return to his native village, and find a solution to the ethical dilemma faced by the community of Madhva brahmins. Praneshacharya thus becomes a symbol of fall without any suggestion of regeneration. He is more and more hardened by the non-brahminical demonic world to accept his desecration of brahminical values. He, thus, tries to escape from the positive world to the negative one. But the whisky priest's life strikes us to be definitely nobler than Praneshacharya's. Though the whisky priest escapes from the agnostic world of the Mexican society and Government, though he has not been the highest embodiment of Catholic ideals, yet he escapes into the religious world itself, by dying for it thereby becoming almost a martyr. He, in spite of his weaknesses, attains the nobility if not the grandeur of a martyr. Graham Greene shows his leanings towards God's party. But Praneshacharya does not show any sign of regeneration as most of his suffering is confined only to psychic level and he never undergoes the whisky priest's physical suffering like being imprisoned, being made to clean the lavatory buckets, being betrayed by the half-caste or being made to be shot dead by the Government in addition to his psychic dilemmas. Praneshacharya is more an observer than a participant, whereas the whisky priest is more a participant than an observer. Anantha Murthy seems to relish the acharya's fall and the hidden *sudra* in Naranappa and Praneshacharya.

The whisky priest, in spite of his falling short of certain ideals of his religion, enlists our sympathy by his nobility of suffering and sacrifice of his life for his faith. Thus Graham Greene's picture of a religious man's rise in spite of his fall, his death in the interest of his faith is indeed very comprehensive and conclusive, whereas Anantha Murthy's picture of Praneshacharya's life is partial and inconclusive because he does not show whether the acharya has taken any decision after the realization of his folly and repentance. The story is left dangling at the end of *Samskara*. Anantha Murthy's philosophy appears to be negative and partial, whereas Graham Greene's is affirmative and comprehensive. That is the reason why the whisky priest's fall and rise assume the importance of an archetypal image whereas the Acharya's fall remains a partial and unconvincing symbol.

Comparatively speaking, the canvas of *The Power and the Glory* is very large, as it encompasses the whole of the Mexican society and Government and the entire Catholic community, whereas that of *Sarnskara* is very narrow as it is confined only to the brahmin, especially Madhva brahmin community having minor bickering with other sub-sects like Smartas and the liberal brahmins of Kundapura. *The Power and the Glory* thus concerns itself with the large entities geographically, politically and religiously, whereas *Samskara* is limited to small entities of life geographically (confined only to Durvasapura, Kundapura and in between villages) and religiously (confined only to sectarian brahmins' dilemmas).

The plot of *The Power and the Glory* is double dimensional in that it can be read both as a thriller on a secular level and as a religious novel. It appeals both to the non-Catholic reader and to the Catholic one. The materialistic triumph of the Mexican Government in hunting out the last priest and killing him by way of punishment also involves the concurrent sacrifice of the priest for his faith or ideal. Thus both the lieutenant (representative of the communist Government) and the whisky priest are triumphant in their own ways. Whereas the Government (State) triumphs over the priest (Church), the priest becomes triumphant by laying down his life for his faith. This kind of double-dimensionality cannot be found in *Samskara* which shows only the triumph of flesh over spirit, instinct over reason, *sudra* tendency over brahminism, and therefore operates only in one dimension.

Both the novels contain some symbolic motifs. Whereas eagles in *The Power and the Glory* symbolize evil and death, vultures in *Samskara* symbolize death and decadent brahminism.

Likewise mosquitoes and malaria hold a mirror to the physical disease and symbolize moral corruption in Mexico, rats and plague reflect the deadliness of the disease and fast rate of morality in the villages around Durvasapura. In both the novels, physical disease complements the moral decadence. Anantha Murthy's description of rats and people dying on account of being inflicted by plague seems to be relatively overdone as he appears to be overtly influenced by Albert Camus' *The Plague*.

One is easily struck by the difference of style in both the novels. The general impression created on the mind of the reader happens to be that the language of *Samskara* appears to be more poetic and picturesque than that of *The Power and the Glory* which is relatively dry and denotes dehydration of emotion which is, perhaps, due to Graham Greene's early training in film-script writing.

Both the novels are based upon actual events that happened in life some time ago. As Graham Greene has mentioned, his whisky priest was partially based upon the life of a hunted priest in Mexico. Similarly, Anantha Murthy has confessed in the Kannada journal *Rujuvatu* that though his Praneshacharya was based upon a real brahmin of south India, he was inspired to write such a novel only after seeing a Russian film in Birmingham.

The comparative study of the two novels has shown us the emergence of a universal pattern i.e. desecration of religious values, in spite of cultural dissimilarities and particularities.

Works Cited

Graham Greene, *The Power and the Glory* (Harmondsworth: Penguin, 1970).

U.R. Anantha Murthy, *Samskara*, trans. A.K. Ramanujan (Delhi: Oxford University Press, 1985).

Samskara: A Window on Brahminic Orthodoxy

N. SONIA
Jiri College, Manipur

U.R. Anantha Murthy's *Samskara* seems to have left no stone unturned in unveiling the hypocrisy of orthodoxy of the brahmin community of South India of the 1930s and 1940s. In fact, it's a big mockery of the South brahmins of those times and Anantha Murthy despite being a brahmin himself unravels the orthodox practices which affected the social environment and brought irreparable doom to the entire sect of the so-called high class brahmin group, the Madhvas. In *Samskara* the plague spreads to the entire agrahara. The novel recounts a sad childhood experience of Anantha Murthy's own agrahara. As the author writes in one of his articles on *Samskara:*

> I was barely 13 years old when some momentous things happened in my little Agrahara. Everyone was talking about an imminent 'Pralaya.' If everyone was going to be destroyed, I thought in my childish innocence, people will be very generous and my parents will not say 'no' to any indulgence of mine. I used to have dreams of rice Roti being eaten in the night previous to the Pralaya with all the honey and ghee my mother had kept locked. Not only Pralaya, but I was also witness to actual death all round me. Four miles away was my high school which was closed because of plague in the town. People began to die along with the rats. In my village only the pariahs died. That was because, I had realized, the orthodox doctor had not gone to inoculate against plague—they were untouchables. Although I was surrounded by all these people, something in me was stirred against all these superstitious beliefs.[1]

The entire story of the novel revolves around the pending death rite of a renegade Brahmin Naranappa because each one of the Madhva brahmins felt that because of Naranappa's wayward libertine ways, his cremation ceremony could not be conducted without consulting the holy books. The most learned Madhva Praneshacharya whom the entire clan looked upon and revered as the 'Crest-Jewel of Vedanta' could not come to an amicable solution. It is indeed a great dilemma for Praneshacharya and the entire sect but it also seems cruel and sinister that a group of the so-called high class brahmins who have read the Vedas and the Puranas are keeping the dead body of a man unburnt and rotting just because they cannot decide whether to cremate it or not, just because he had deviated from the brahminic way of life. Suresh Raval observes: "Orthodox brahminism is vividly presented in Praneshacharya's fruitless search for an answer from the scriptures, and it is made even more simple-mindedly ritualistic and superstitious by his prayers to Lord Maruti for divine intercession."[2]

Orthodoxy looms large in the woop and warp of the novel. At the very beginning of the novel, Chandri, the lower caste woman that Naranappa lived with, comes to inform Praneshacharya about the death of Naranappa. The unreasonableness of and ugly orthodox belief in the caste divide is laid bare as Chandri's voice rings in the ears of everyone. If the Acharya talked to her, he would be polluted; he'd have to bathe again before his meal.[3]

Talking to Chandri means that the brahmin has to take another bath to purify himself. This clearly shows the casteism that existed then and would later on engulf the entire society. The irony is that these high class brahmins fall flat right on their noses as they are unable to keep up their set rules and succumb to the very human shortcomings of greed and lust which they despise in the members of the inferior sections.

When the discussion of Naranappa's funeral was going on each one of these Brahmins poured out his hatred and disgust at the dead man's unbrahminic ways. Even Gurdacharya who was Naranappa's own kinsman talked menacingly against Naranappa's keeping a lower caste woman for his mistress in the very presence of the poor woman. Obviously, he was bent on insulting Chandri. As he said: "Let's set aside the question of whether I should do the rites. The real question is: is he a brahmin at all? What do you say? He slept regularly with a lower caste woman." (5)

Gurdacharya's charges were, however, funnily countered by Durgabhatta, the only Smarta brahmin in the agrahara among the Madhvas and who was always checking the rival sect's orthodoxy. As he said:

> Chi Chi Chi, don't be too rash, Acharya. O no, a brahmin isn't lost because he takes a lowborn prostitute. Our ancestors after all came from the North—you can ask Praneshacharya if you wish—history says they cohabited with Dravidian women. Don't think I am facetious. Think of all the people who go to the brothels of Basrur in South Canara. (5)

These brahmins are lusty men who hide their inner carnal desires behind the pious visage of a brahmin inside the walls of the agrahara. But once they are out to some faraway place they take every opportunity to fulfil their biological urge. Here, the question is, where is the pollution gone? They are shown as cheap, double-faced cheats. The pollution caused by merely talking to a lowcaste woman is nothing compared to physically touching such a woman, but all these issues become trifling matters to a wandering brahmin as soon as he crosses the precincts of his agrahara.

The entire agrahara is shown going all out to throw brickbats at Naranappa after his death which they were unable to do when he was alive. In the words of Lakshmanacharya:

> I am not the sort who would hide anything about him just because he was my close relative. He was my wife's uncle's son. We tolerated things and sheltered him in our lap as long as we could. In return, what does he do? He comes to the river in full view of all the brahmins and takes the holy stone that we've worshipped for generations and throws it in the water and spites after it. Condone everything if you wish—but didn't he, wilfully, before our very eyes, bring Muslims over and in the wide open frontyard, eat and drink forbidden things? If any of us questioned him, in good faith, he would turn on us, cover us with abuse from head to foot. As long as he lived, we just had to walk in fear of him. (7)

It is funny to see that this so-called high class group flex their muscles only when the disobedient and the fearful outcast brahmin Naranappa is no more. This also shows the weakness of their belief, their fear, their lack of firmness. Had there been two Naranappas they would all have seen their brahminic orthodoxy trampled to pieces.

Another interesting point in this novel is the mocking exposure of the greediness of the brahmins such as their greediness for free sumptuous meals—and their fear that they might not be invited to such meals if they hurriedly performed the death rites of Naranappa without consulting the holy books:

> Dasacharya lived entirely on the meals that brahmins get at death rites and anniversaries. He would walk ten miles for such a meal any day. 'As you all know, we let him stay in our agrahara, so for two whole years we didn't get calls for any meal or banquet. If we do the rites for him now or anything rash like that, no one will ever invite us for a brahmin meal.' (7-8)

As the novel depicts, to the brahmins free meals are more important than cremating the body of a fellow brahmin. Again, as is customary the brahmins cannot take their meal until the dead body is cremated. As such, excluding their children the entire brahmin sect were starved for days. At this crucial juncture, Dasacharya, unable to suppress his hunger, went to Parijatapura, the place of the lower clan of Brahmins whom the Madhvas looked down upon and despised because of their less orthodox outlook:

> Unseen by anyone, he went to the waters of the Tunga river, bathed in the burning sun and walked towards Parijatapura. He soon stood in the shade of Manjayya's thatched canopy. How could he ask here openely for food? In all his born days, he hadn't touched water in the houses of these crosslined brahmins. After all, he was a brahmin who lived on ritual meals. Bad things will happen if others hear about. . . . Dasacharya stood there in a trance, looking only at the uppittu. (53-54)

When Manjayya offered him food, he pretended being afraid of his agrahara people coming to know about it and the consequence thereof. As he says: "I dont really mind eating in your house. But if those rascals in our agrahara hear about it, no one will invite me to a ceremony again. What can I do, Manjayya?" (55) Further, when he starts eating he makes some more funny gestures: "Dasacharya rubbed his belly to the name of the supreme spirit, and didn't say No. Just for courtesy's sake, he pretended to cover his eating leaf with his hands, . . . 'Enough. Enough. Must leave some for you.'" (56)

Dasacharya's eating at Manjayya's house is hilarious indeed, bringing out the greed and weakness of brahmins for good food in utter disregard of the brahminic need for austerity. Another instance of greediness of these brahmins is when they greedily eye Chandri's gold jewellery, which she takes out and places in front of the entire sect as a price for having Naranappa's body cremated:

> The women calculated swiftly: that heap of gold was worth at least two thousand rupees. One after another, the wives scanned their husbands' faces. The brahmins bowed their heads: they were afraid, fearful that the lust for gold might destroy brahmin purity. But in the heart of every one of them flashed the question: if some other brahmin should perform the final rite for Naranappa, he might keep his brahminhood and yet put all that gold on his wife's neck. (9-10)

As gold is desired by everybody, so is it by brahmins. After catching sight of Chandri's gold, Lakshmanacharya and Garudacharya see little reason for an argument as to who should be allowed to do the cremation. In fact, this is a show of their human weakness no matter how far they may feign their disinterestedness in these worldly desires. How far can one renounce material desires? And for that matter how far can they go in attempting or practising at renouncing physical desires? It is just impossible. After all the holy Hindu scriptures are full of lusty stories of Gods and Godesses and this is also one strong reason for the young brahmin youths gathering in front of Praneshacharya's house every evening. The brahmins are no models of material renunciation nor of physical renunciation. One incident to support this point is when Praneshacharya decides to give up telling the luscious puranic stories of Shakuntala and Menaka out of disgust because Naranappa had accused him once.

> 'You read those lush sexy puranas, but you preach a life of barenness.' He gave up telling the luscious puranic stories in the evenings and started on moral tales of penance. The result—his own enthusiasm for reciting the puranas faded and died. The young listenners who used to look at him with lively eyes and bring joy to his heart—they stopped coming. Only women bent on earning merit, uttering the names of god over yawns in the middle of the stories, and old men, were his audience now. (25)

It is saddening to see these religious, God-fearing men starving for food for days just because a fellow brahmin's body remains uncremated. Praneshacharya's strong faith in the supreme God and Madhva brahmins' faith in Praneshacharya, the Crest-Jewel of Vedanta is indeed remarkable. In the name of God they bear hardship of every brahminic law without once raising a finger against its rather unwelcome disciplining at times. But in the end everything collapses. Dasacharya's breaking of his fast on the sly is example enough to show the breaking up of the rigidness of brahminic laws. Even though everyone despised Naranappa, it is Naranappa's ways that they follow knowingly or unknowingly. Praneshacharya who tried his best to bring back the brahminic way of life faces failure and in the long run he too fails to live up to his status of a pious brahmin, despite being himself the best of his entire sect. All his life he had tended tirelessly his invalid wife and kept himself far from the carnal world and yet he was happy with his lot. He felt his marrying an invalid and serving her was one of his greatest achievements as a pious brahmin on his path to salvation as is depicted in the very beginning of the novel:

> Didn't Lord Krishna say: Do what's to be done with no thought of fruit? The Lord definitely means to test him on his way to salvation; that's why He's given him a brahmin birth this time and set him up in this kind of family. The Acharya is filled with pleasure . . . he is filled with ccompassion for his ailing wife. He proudly swells a little at his lot, thinking, 'By marrying an invalid, I get ripe and ready.' (2)

But later after he sleeps with Chandri in the darkness of the forest he wants to throw away his brahminic ways. He feels guilty of his act, of his inability to control his sexual urge and indulging himself in the arms of the lowcaste woman. But it is the human in him which had made him act in that manner. All his brahminic philosophy undergoes a sudden change after that experience. He wants to be with Chandri again and even starts fantasizing about other lowcaste women:

> He remembered the darkness in which Chandri had fed him the plaintains from her lap. . . . He'd heard that a young lad went to the river bank and slept with an outcaste girl there, after hearing his description of Shakuntala. The Acharya's fantasy dragged in all the untouchable girls he'd never thought of; stripped them and looked at them. (79)

The novel is on the realistic plane as it shows sexual desire of a normal man leaping out of Praneshacharya fiercely with a vengeance. All his long suppressed desires erupt like a powerful volcano. All vows of celibacy are thrown to the winds. Thus the attempt of a holy brahmin to trudge the path of celibacy is nothing except hypocrisy and an exercise in futility.

The final and the most lethal blow to orthodoxy is the spread of plague in the agrahara after Naranappa dies of it. Not even once do the brahmins try to know the cause of his death. They look utterly ignorant even after rats come out of their holes dying right in front of their eyes in all the brahmin houses. They think only of Naranappa's death rite which remains undecided despite a lot of discussion and arguments. Naranappa had in fact died of plague which he contacted from Shivamogge and since his dead body lay uncremated it was very natural for the rats to eat and die of it and spread the plague to the entire agrahara. Naranappa's death was followed by Dasacharya's and then Praneshacharya's wife's and a host of others. In the untouchables' colony too people were dying of plague and the huts were set on fire along with the dead bodies.

The once proud Brahmins are helpless in the hands of a deadly disease. Their ignorance of medical science has made them an easy prey to plague. It is disheartening that none of them even contemplates about consulting a doctor except the one thoughtful, outgoing brahmin Manjayya of Parijatapur who shows some understanding. The moment he hears of the rats running out of the agrahara and dying in Durvasapura he quickly warns his fellow brahmins to take safety measures. He even arranges to go immediately to inform the municipality to get Naranappa's dead body removed, calls in doctors and gets everybody inoculated. He arranges for rat exterminators and pumps. The orthodox Madhvas are left at their wits' end. They are utterly dejected and hopeless:

> They walked with a heavy heart to Kaimara and what did they see? Dasacharya's cremated ashes, the news of the death of Praneshacharya's wife. They were bewildered. Their familiar world was in confusion. They felt they'd seen demons in the dark. Like children they leaned on walls, tears flowing from their eyes. (103)

The brahmins are shaken by the menace of the plague. Had they been a little cautious and a little bit aware of modern medicine and a little large-hearted, they would not have faced the catastrophe. Throughout the novel the need to fight brahminic orthodoxy is clearly visible. Anantha Murthy's voice calling for a new life sans the evils of brahminhood is echoed. As Dunkin Jalki points out:

> The solution to the orthodoxy of brahminism and its resultant casteism thus basically involves giving up all kinds of rituals and practices traditionally associated with brahminism. Praneshacharya, after a disappointment with brahaminism, does what Naranappa did for years; wanders through forests and lonely roads, sleeps with the prostitute Chandri, thinks of sleeping with another, visits fairs and cockfights, and eats in a temple in an unclean condition. Despite all these, a sad realization haunts him: "he may have rejected brahminhood, but brahminhood never left him". As a matter of fact, Praneshacharya makes this statement about Naranappa. Nevertheless, very soon he finds himself trapped in this truth. It goes without saying that this realization is not just of Praneshacharya but also that of the author.[4]

Jalki further adds, quoting Anantha Murthy himself as in the following lines: "Anantha Murthy does not shy away from accepting that he criticizes brahmins. "Hurting brahmins for me born and brought up as a brahmin, is not an issue that I like, but is inevitable. My writings like *Samskara*, 'Ghatashraddha,' Bharatipura, have hurt brahmins. . . .What I've written are the essential truth that brahmins must face". (181)

Anantha Murthy's mocking representation of brahminhood and its orthodoxy in *Samskara* may no doubt have offended the brahmin communities of the south. As A.K. Ramanujan writes in Afterword of his English translation of the novel: "Certain Brahmin communities in South India were offended by the picture of decadent brahminism. They felt that brahmin men and women were unfairly caricatured; they were offended by the novelist's rather intrusive partiality for Naranappa and the Sudra women." (143-44)

Samskara must have hurt the sentiments of the South Indian Brahmin community to a considerable extent but Muthy's work could prove of immense benefit to the brahmin community. The author has come out with a very realistic rendering of the evil practices of the highly orthodox Brahmin community of the South and his fearless presentation of the orthodoxy-ridden community with all its flaws and worthlessness is indeed a priceless effort which has cut through the barriers of language, religion, sex and caste, making the novel the most readable, thought-provoking and unforgettable window on the life of the orthodox brahmins of South India.

NOTES.

1. U.R. Anantha Murthy, "How I Wrote *Samskara*," in Kailash C. Baral, D. Venkat Rao and Sura P. Rath, ed., *U.R. Anantha Murthy's "Samskara": A Critical Reader*, p. 69.
2. Suresh Raval, *Interpreting Cultural Impasse in Anantha Murthy's Samskara*, in Baral, Venkat Rao and Sura P. Rath, ed., p. 117.
3. Qtd. U.R. Anantha Murthy, *Samskara*, trans. A.K. Ramanujan (Delhi: OUP, 1976), p. 2.
4. Dunkin Jalki, "Orientalism as linguistic Behavior: On Anti-Brahmin Rhetoric of *Samskara*," in Baral, et al, ed., p. 191.

Samskara: A Critique of Hinduism

MADHUMITA GANGULI
Christ Church College, Kanpur

'Dharma' imposes rules of moral action in the form of categorical imperatives or simply presents certain examples of virtue that in turn guide the formulation of the rules of action and Karma. In this context let us define 'Dharma,' morality and virtue vis-a-vis moral conduct and misconduct, some key issues taken up in Anantha Murthy's *Samskara*. The centrality of the concept of "Dharma" in the ethical religious and social sense as present in India, stands in the relation to character, as Bimal Matilal suggests that the world is 'the field where the seeds of moral merit / demerit are sown in order to bring forth the harvest of Karma or just a moral desert.'[1] The broad implication of this suggestion seems to be that question of moral 'rightness' or 'wrongness' which is encompassed in the complex notion of 'Dharma.' Granting centrality to "Dharma" in Indian tradition, this concept eludes any ready interpretation in terms of prevailing criteria of ethical theory. It generally sets itself the task of coming up with codes consisting of universal rules or principles. These rules or principles amount to a decision procedure for determining what is the right action in any particular case. This is the problem which Praneshacharya confronts in *Samskara*.

The morality of 'Dharma' is derived from the conduct of virtuous people and the idea of being a virtuous person, whose conduct is governed by "prajna" (practical wisdom) which is embodied in Mahajana (good conduct). The virtue of 'Dharma' cannot be equated merely with a set of universal moral rules for the application in actual contexts of practical life. Appreciating the meaning of 'Dharma' in terms of its situation in a 'higher' order and therefore its 'reigning from above' over the phenomenal order of practical life, helps to explain the difference which exists between 'Dharma' and moral rules. While moral rules are directly applied to particular contexts of actual life, these rules depend for their normative content on ideals and truths of abstract and general nature. The embodiment of these ideals and truths constitute virtues, and one might say that an idealized image of virtuous personhood is what is depicted as 'Dharma.' It is in this sense, that 'Dharma' 'proposes' from higher, transcendental order the ideal norms that are adopted and shaped into codifiable moral rules for the purpose of their application in the living contexts of life. In essence, the claim might be that moral rules are abstractions from the density and depth of virtues laid out in the 'dharmic' order.

One of the major sources of knowledge about 'dharmic' order is in the ancient scriptures which are viewed as the repository of practical wisdom or 'prajna.' The great epics and legends and mythologies portray different aspects of 'dharmic' reality and practical wisdom. It would seem from this that the quality of being virtuous in the actual course of human life is measured by the degree to which our mortal life tends to approximate the image of perfection. A majority of Indians believe in this doctrine, and the concomitant doctrine of Karma, that man is reborn in happy or unhappy conditions according to his actions. His evil actions will result in inevitable suffering. In priestly codes there is a tendency to confuse virtue with ceremonial purity, to kill a man is bad, but to touch his corpse is worse. The great scriptures disregard technical morality and insist on the spirit of self-control and love of humanity. To be able to fulfill the obligations expected of man he must exercise self-control. Not only what we accept but what we renounce contributes to our making. Threefold is the gate to hell that destroys the self: lust, anger and greed. We must fight against these with the weapons of the spirit, favouring chastity to lust, love to anger, and generosity to greed. The *Mahabharata* says, 'The rules of 'Dharma' or virtuous conduct taught by the great sages, each of whom relied on his own illumination, are manifold. The highest among them all is self-control.' (*San-*

tiparva, Cl iv, 6) It is for developing self-control that austerities and asceticism are practised, but when real self-control is attained these rigorous practices are unnecessary. Insistence on discipline or self-control avoids the two extremes of self-indulgence and asceticism.

Discipline of the soul does not mean either the starving of the senses or the indulgence of them (*Bhagawat Gita*, vi, 16-18). The world is not only spiritual but also moral. Life is an education. In the moral sphere whatever man 'soweth that shall he reap.' The law of morality is fundamental to the cosmic order. 'Our own deeds bring to us their fruits' (Garuda Purana). The law of karma holds that man can create his future by creating in the present what will produce the desired effect. Man is the sole master of his fate. But so long as he is the victim of his desires and allows his activities to be governed by automatic attractions and repulsions he is not exercising his freedom. If chains fetter us, they are of our own forging and we ourselves may rend them asunder. God works by persuasion rather than by force. Right and wrong is not the same thing and the choice we make is a real one. All the battles of tradition and defiance, asceticism and sensuality, the meaning and meaninglessness of ritual, 'Dharma' as nature and law, desire (kama) and salvation (Moksha) become internalized in the soul of Praneshacharya. The conflict lies in the body and the spirit of the protagonist, seeking an answer. Praneshacharya's Brahminism questions itself in a modern existential mode. In search of an answer he treads into the world of Chandri, Naranappa and Putta. He comes to know of such experiences, which he had never known earlier, which gives him a wholeness or completeness of experience, in the end he has gained knowledge hitherto unknown to him.

The problem of good and evil, sin, suffering and sorrow is perhaps the oldest question in the history of human kind. This issue has been argued and discussed by philosophers and thinkers without reaching satisfactory conclusion, ever since the concepts of moral values and ideals came into being, and it remains incomprehensible and unanswerable even to the present day. Anantha Murthy's award winning novel *Samskara* explores this eternal question seeking an answer, which causes existential crisis and moral dilemma in the mind of the protagonist. Set in the early twentieth century India, the book depicts how thin the demarcating line is between the so-called conflicting values as defined and viewed by society. Durvasapura lends a microcosmic view of Hinduism as practised in India. The Brahmin orthodoxies are repeatedly questioned in the reformist climate of the 1930s and 40s with Gandhi's teaching and the ideas of secularism becoming prevalent. Vedantic thought and Hinduism needed to be changed to fit the present needs. The Brahmin, as the highest in the social ranking, must at all times be ritually pure since he was the priest and the spokesman of the community, he intercedes with the gods, so he must remain pure. The Brahmin was the keeper of the sacred traditions and the Vedas, which he had, for two thousand years, preserved, interpreted and transmitted. As the keeper of the Hindu traditions, the Brahmins once upon a time wielded great powers and were looked up to by the other castes, but as time progressed and with modernization the Brahmin power dwindled. *Samskara* shows the general denuding of values and morality among the Brahmins.

The novel is set against the backdrop of death. An attack of plague ravages Durvasapura and Shivamogge. The atmosphere is filled with stench of rotting flesh and vultures preying on dead rats. The novel begins with the news of the death of a rebelling member of an orthodox clan of Brahmins, who lived in the 'agraharam' of Durvasapura. He dies of plague. Naranappa is the black sheep of the 'agrahara': he scandalizes the entire community by indulging openly in meat eating, wine and women and dies issueless. None of the Brahmins of the 'agrahara' come forward to perform his last rites as they considered it against Hindu scriptures to cremate a man who had sullied Brahminism and stepped out of it. They seek the advice of Praneshacharya, the most respected person, and the spiritual guide of the inhabitants of the 'agrahara.' Naranappa advocates hedonistic ways of life. He does not believe in practising the rituals, which a normal Brahmin was expected to do. He went against Brahminism and turned into a heretic. He treated Brahmins with contempt and preferred to keep the company of Muslims, he says, "All your Brahmin respectability, I'll roll it up and throw it away for a little bit of pleasure with one female." (21) He defies every Brahminic rule, he abandoned his Brahmin wife "who in the world can live with a girl who gives no pleasure" (20) and started living with an outcaste woman Chandri, who he had brought from Kundapura. He ate and drank 'forbidden things' (7)—meat, fish, liquor, he flung the holy stone, sacred to Vishnu, and worshipped by the Brahmins, into the Tunga River and spat on it. He caught the fish in the sacred tank of the temple with his Muslim friends. He could not be excommunicated because he threatened to become a Muslim. If he had really become a Muslim, the Brahmins of Durvasapura would have had no option, but to leave the 'agraharam,' to escape pollution. Lakshmanacharya says: "If he had really become a Muslim, no law could have thrown him out of the Brahmin agraharam. We would have to leave." (11)

Even in death Naranappa becomes an enemy of the Brahmins. His plague-infested body rots and evinces a stench since none of the Brahmins would come forward to perform his last rites for fear of sullying their caste. The entire 'agraharam' is threatened by the epidemic which Naranappa contracted in Shivamogge, ultimately a Muslim cremates his body at the request of Chandri. It was considered a sin for a Brahmin to be cremated by any one other than a Brahmin, if he died without an offspring. Even though she offered her gold ornaments none of the Brahmins came forward to cremate the body. Praneshacharya failed to give a decision in this case.

Praneshacharya 'the Crest-Jewel of Vedic Learning' was unable to come up with a solution about how to dispose the corpse of Naranappa. Neither the scriptures nor the Maruti idol in the temple where he prayed for an answer offered any solution. When he came out of the temple in utter despair, unable to take a decision and was walking home, he encountered Chandri, the low-caste mistress of Naranappa in the forest. In a moment of weakness his flesh gave in to Chandri. This episode changed his life, and marked a turning point in the story and in his character.

The protagonist faces two situations of a possible radical existential crisis. The first occurs in his youth when, studying in

Benaras, he had encountered Mahabala, who had been his friend and classmate and was a promising student. Later he found him living his life with a prostitute, and changing his course of life altogether, giving up priesthood. Later, as a priest. Praneshacharya also met Naranappa, a reckless, dissolute person to whom "Dharma", virtue, morality meant nothing, who had always believed in materialistic hedonistic pleasures of the world with no fears of the hereafter. His encounter with Mahabala earlier had driven Pranesh to a deeper religious orthodoxy. He married an invalid woman Bhagirathi, and lived a life of celibacy and asceticism. Thus far in his life he had made conscious choices in order to be a firm representative of high religious ideals and orthodox Hinduism. Praneshacharya's fruitless search for an answer in the scriptures, and in the ritualistic and superstitious prayers to lord Maruti in the temple, for a miraculous solution to his problem, failing in both he lost control, he lost his 'prajna' and 'mahajana' and stepped into the dark world of sin. He is haunted by sin trying to run away from himself. The question that arises here is, is merely moral conduct Dharma? A sincere repentance could be the atonement of sin. His meeting and fulfillment of his repressed desires, which an invalid wife could never give him, gives a new angle to his life and to the narrative. His morality is wiped away in a moment as he falls prey to his pent-up desires, "Orthodox Brahminism is virtually presented in Praneshacharya's fruitless search for an answer from the scriptures, and it is made even more simple mindedly ritualistic and superstitious by his prayers to Lord Maruti for divine intervention." (177) Praneshacharya goes through a crisis in his life at this juncture. Chandri after having cremated Naranappa with the help of Ahmad Bari goes away to Kundapura. She makes an exit and does not appear in the novel again. She leaves behind her a devastated man whose entire life changes and enters into a new phase. His soul becomes an arena of conflict and search for an answer. Praneshacharya who so far had embodied balance, restraint, thoughtfulness and universality grounded in Vedantic thoughts and practice, all these virtues are thrown into disarray in a moment when he experiences Chandri, just after his fruitless struggle to find an answer. Other Brahmins of the 'agrahara' are greedy, selfish and corrupt. Naranappa was reckless, defiant, he consorted with low caste men and women, and lived with a prostitute with no pangs of conscience. He was married to the sister of Lakshmanacharya's wife who got hysterical and died because of Naranappa's misbehaviour.

Irresolution is central to the novel, there is a dualism, which seems existential in nature. Praneshcharya goes through a crisis in his life, when he commits a moral transgression which results in his abasement and loss of 'self.' He does not remain the same man, proud of his asceticism the 'Crest-Jewel of Vedantic Learning.' He fell prey to his passion momentarily, but the guilt haunts him. Then Putta comes in his life when he is crumbling in a 'trishanku' state under the weight of moral crisis, and takes him to Padmavati, another attractive low-caste woman who reminds him of Matsyagandhi who had caste a spell on Rishi Parashara and out of the illicit liaison was born Vyas, the creator of the *Mahabharata.*

This facinating novel has for its background the darkness of death looming large with vultures preying on dead rats, people dying of plague. This valley of death represents the world. In it there are men of all kinds, men who suffer the fruits of their Karma. Anantha Murthy brings in the thoughts of Charvaka, represented by Naranappa, and the Yoga School of thought represented by Praneshacharya, and the concept of Sankhya of Purush and Prakriti believed by the Madhva sect. There is a search for wholeness for a complete experience of the desires and its fulfillment. Celibacy and ascetism do not give completeness to the life of Praneshacharya. Putta shows him the darker side of life, good and evil together constitute the fullest experience of life. Pranesh had not experienced an important part of life, he was incomplete till Chandri showed him the passions which he had never experienced before, which after experiencing he had to conquer like the sages, Vishwamitra and Parashara. Praneshacharya's journey, is a journey towards self-realization, a complete knowledge of the world of good and evil.

The novel also delves into the complexities of 'Dharma,' virtue and morality, vis-à-vis sin and evil. Sages like Shankara, Durvasa and Vishwamitra had conquered the 'self.' They had sucked the honey of life, yet obtained the state of Sthitipragya. The soul journeys from 'prajna' (practical wisdom) to Mahajana (complete wisdom of good conduct) ultimately achieves 'moksha,' freedom from all bondage. Pranesh's journey is like the journey which Gautam Buddha had taken and seen the suffering in life which made him renounce the world. Whatever Praneshacharya did was not of his own choice, it happened to him unintentionally, or was compelled by forces outside him. The novel is a complex novel with a deep touch of Indian ethics which holds the key to the problem of Pranesh: 'Even if I leave everything behind, the community clings to me, asking me to fulfill duties the Brahmin is born to do. It is not easy to free one's self of this.' 'Shall I tell him I have sinned and lost the chance of penance?' 'I'm absolutely not responsible for making love to her. Not responsible for that moment. But the moment altered me—Why?' But he yearns for the touch again. 'Now if I go in search of her, and enjoyed her, I would be fully responsible for my act, wouldn't I?' He couldn't return to the 'agrahara' because of fear, he could not live with a lie. Naranappa had 'kicked away at Brahminism,' lived a life of sin and died. Now his corpse lay facing a crisis whether any Brahmin was entitled to perform his death rite since he was issueless, and lead an unbrahminical life. No Brahmin would pollute himself by performing his death rite. Second problem was, then who would do it since he had not been excommunicated, and a Brahmin was 'twice-born,' so it was essential to give him a proper cremation or his soul would become a 'brahma daitya' and this would to do more harm to the community, which was a superstition the Brahmins believed in.

The problem taken up in this novel is moral transgression and sin. The novelist tries to analyze the eternal problems of sin, morality virtues and 'Dharma,' by various illustrations from the epics and the lives of the sages, Vishwamitra was seduced by Maneka, Parashara by Matsyagadhi, but they did not face a moral dilemma like Pranesh. Shankara was challenged by a woman philosopher, so he experienced sex within a king's body which he had entered. Pranesh deviates from the path of morality. Naranappa violates morality and the rest of the Brahmins of the agrahara had fallen into evil ways of greed yet adhered to the superstitions and rituals. Pranesh was morally conscious of his guilt, and did not know how to resolve it, thus the struggle between 'Dharma' and 'Karma,' the latter overcomes the former and takes possession of Praneshacharya.

After Chandri's departure Praneshacharya's initiation to the materialistic world is taken up by Putta, the simple villager, who goes all out to help him on the way, by selling his silver coin, taking him to the temple fair to watch the cock fight, and from there to the prostitute Padmavati. Putta takes him to eat at the temple feast. Pranshacharya felt guilty, as he should not be eating within the temple, at the festival when he was in the polluted state, after the death of his wife. He should not have sat with other Brahmins knowing it was ritualistically wrong to eat in the temple. When the man who was serving food recognized him, he got up and fled in fear of discovery. His guilt haunted him everywhere. He could not be like Mahabala who was bold enough to give up his priesthood and live with a prostitute. He could not be like Naranappa who lived in sin till death. He measured himself against the sages of yore who gave in to the passions, and yet were above it, and men like Mahabala and Naranappa, who did not experience a duality nor pangs of conscience. Praneshacharya goes back to Durvasapura, on a cart with a rich man with a heavy heart and conscience to face the other Brahmins of Durvasapura. But he would neither confess, nor atone for his sins, he would merely tell them the truth. The novelist ends with an underlying question, as to what then could be the path that leads to morality, virtue and 'Dharma.'

NOTES

1. U.R. Anantha Murthy, *Samskara*, trans. A.K. Ramanujan (New York and Oxford: Oxford University Press, 1978).
2. See A.K. Ramanujan, "Afterword," *Samskara*, pp. 145-46
3. A.L. Bashiam, *A Cultural History of India* (New York and Oxford: Oxford University Press 1975), pp. 114-23.
4. Nirad C. Chaudhuri, *Hinduism a Religion to Live By* (New York and Oxford: Oxford University Press, 1979), pp. 198-200.
5. Barbara Stoler Miller, ed., *Masterpieces of Asian Literature in Comparqtive Perspective* (New York: M.E. Sharpe), pp. 189-200.

Social Pressure vs. Individual Consciousness: A Study of *Samskara*

MONIKA GUPTA
H.N.B. University, Srinagar Garhwal

Indian literature written in regional languages is so rich and diversified that not only in India but people from all over the world are reading and appreciating it. Winner of Jnanapeeth Award in 1994, for his novel *Samskara* (1965), Udupi Rajagopala Acharya Anantha Murthy was born in 1932 at Melige, a remote village in Tirthalli Taluk, in Shimoga district. In literary field he is known for his poems, stories, essays and novels. His novel *Samskara* was translated by A.K. Ramanujan in 1976 in English. Apart from English, *Samskara* has been translated into Russian, German, Hungarian, French, Swedish, Hindi, Bengali, Malayalam, Marathi, Urdu, Tamil and Gujarati. Set in rural area in South India, where people are strictly divided according to traditional caste system, the novel deals with the death of Naranappa, who is involved in the activities which are against the norms of Brahminism; dilemma of Praneshacharya, the most respectable priest of the Agrahara; and miserable condition of Chandri, concubine of Naranappa. As far as the theme of the novel is concerned, Anantha Murthy has skillfully portrayed Brahmin-Dalit conflict, problems of superstitions in uneducated Indian villagers, and marginalisation of women in Indian social system.

According to Manu, *Samskara* purifies the body. Some of the important *Samskaras* are *Garbhadhan*, *punsvana*, *jatkarma*, *namkarna*, *upnayana*, *samavartana*, *vivaha*, *antyesti* etc. From birth to death every Hindu follows these age-old *Samskaras*. The reason is not individual good, but they represent his responsibility to society. Within this process, the balance and harmony of individual and society is maintained. The novel raises the social issues not only in terms of religion and belief but humanistic and moral approach of the characters towards evil, social taboos and sin. In opening scene, Chandri comes to Praneshacharya to inform about the death of Naranappa. But to have conversation with a pure Brahmin is a kind of sin for her. So, she thinks:

> If the Acharya talked to her, he would be polluted; he would have to bathe again before his meal. But how can a morsel go down the gullet with a woman waiting in the yard. (2)

This kind of attitude towards dalits is a very common factor in Indian society. After knowing about the death of Naranappa from Chandri, Praneshacharya rushes to meet Garudacharya, a close relative of Naranappa. Anantha Murthy has described minute details of different kinds of restrictions and norms on the death of someone in the village. Garudacharya is the relative of Naranappa for five generations, and he has to follow the rules set by their ancestors and forefathers. He says to his wife: "It's all right for the children. They can eat. Only we adults shouldn't, till the funeral rites are done." (3)

The news of Naranappa's death spreads like fire. All the villagers gather to take decision about his cremation. It is a social problem for the people of Agrahara which causes dissatisfaction, suffering and misery. Praneshacharya speaks: "Naranappa's death rites have to be done: that's problem one. He has no children. Someone should do it: that's problem two." (4)

Nobody is interested in performing the rites for Naranappa because he "slept regularly with a lowcaste woman," "he even ate what she cooked," "besides drinking, he ate animal flesh." (8) The sins committed by Naranappa are now hindrances in his cremation. Praneshacharya is not able to come to any conclusion. Naranappa had defied every taboo and abandoned his Brahmin wife. An extreme form of punishment for public crime is often banishment from the society. Thinking about Naranappa's overruling tendency of religion and morality, Praneshacharya now thinks about Dharma and Brahminism. *Dharma* covers the way of life of all the creatures created by the nature in this world. He thinks about Naranappa: "For one thing, he may have rejected Brahminhood, but Brahminhood never left him. No one ever excommunicated him officially. He didn't die an outcaste; so he remains a Brahmin in his death. Only another Brahmin has any right to touch his body. If we let someone else do it, we'd be sullying our Brahminhood." (9)

Prevailing rigidity in caste system in Indian social structure is an important aspect of the novel. Under Hinduism, the Hindu community is divided into four classes, Brahmin, Kshatriya, Vaisya and Shudra. Caste system has been the bane of Indian society. In ancient times this division was based on *Karma* not on *Janma*. In Hindu society, the classes under Brahminical order practise their system of faith in accordance with Vedas, Puranas and other related literature. The primary function of the Brahmin caste is to perform various religious and ceremonial rituals. In order to establish the authority of their systems of faiths more rigorously and in an effective manner Brahminical system of faith created rigid and complicated Karamkands. The major problem in the Agrahara is not the issue of cremation of Naranappa, but they are more concerned about their existing values and traditions. Every Brahmin is scared to go against the orthodox system of society. As the most intelligent and sensible man, it is the duty of Praneshacharya to guide, supervise, conduct and restrict the individual behaviour within the orbit of his caste group and in relation to other caste groups.

Dalit movement was active in India in the entire Bhakti movement. Poets like Kabir, Nanak and Ravidas were literary, political and social activists, who worked throughout their life for the welfare of dalits. Post-Independence Indian writers also took this issue very seriously through their writings. On one hand Anantha Murthy has presented strict and rigid norms of Brahminhood, on the other through the character of Chandri he has presented the other side of the coin i.e. problems and marginalisation of dalits.

After the verdict of Praneshacharya, suddenly Chandri gets up and offers all her ornaments as the expense of the cremation of Naranappa. Praneshacharya requests Garuda or Lakshmana to cremate the body. Because Naranappa has no son they are the closest relatives, who can perform the rites. But nobody is interested in performing the rites. Now instead of Brahminism their greedy wives are thinking about the gold offered by Chandri. Rituals help to remind the individual of the holy realm, to revivify and strengthen faith in this realm. Praneshacharya thinks about rituals which say: "Until the body is properly removed there can be no worship, no bathing, no prayers, no food, nothing." (14)

Another Brahmin, Dasacharya suggests that Naranappa was very friendly with the Brahmins of Parijatpura. If the people from Parijatpura are ready to perform the rite, their problem of cremation will be solved and the entire gold will also be with the close relatives of Naranappa. The final decision of cremation is left with Praneshacharya.

Most of the Indian writers have used mythical and legendary stories in their works. The *Ramayana* and the *Mahabharata*, two famous epics of Indian origin, are not only part of our religion, but life's philosophy and morality behind them influence every human being. Anantha Murthy's effort to save Hinduism and Brahminism through the villagers of Agrahara is a forward step in this direction. Like the *Mahabharata*, Anantha Murthy's concept of creating faith and belief in social norms is not by force or terror, rather he tries to conceptualize between theory of religion and Dharma. On one hand Dharma covers the way of life of all the creatures created by nature in the world. It also leads to Brahmin realization which is impossible without moral upliftment. In Indian culture the word Dharma includes the performance of rites, but it further comprehends cultural organization and spirituality. Apart from this it has been equated with self-knowledge. On the other hand Religion is a system of faith created by the various incarnations, prophets and angels from time to time.

The early name of Agrahara was Durvasapura. Tunga River, which flows right in the middle of Agrahara, is supposed to be related to sage Durvasa. It is also believed that during their stay in forest Pandavas stayed for sometime in Kaimara. Once Draupadi desires to swim in that river and in order to fulfill his wife's wish Bheema dammed up the water. Next morning Durvasa became angry and Dharamraja requested Bheema to do something. Bheema broke the dam in three places for proper flow of the water. This legendary story is still alive in Agrahara.

Praneshacharya has promised Naranappa's dying mother to take proper care of him. But when he tries to counsel him, Naranappa's reply makes him desperate:

> Your texts and rites don't worry any more. The Congress Party is coming to power; you'll have to open up the temples to all outcastes. (21)

This statement of Naranappa forces readers to think whether he was really bad or he deliberately wanted to break the taboos and norms made by the society? There are several instances where Praneshacharya tried to counsel him but every time Naranappa made him angry and insulted him by ignoring morality and tradition of Brahminism. Religion and morality are the most influential forces of social control. The Hindu caste system is looked upon as divine institution. People who violate it are considered sinners and it is believed that God will punish them. Due to this internal fear people do not have the courage to violate the laws of the caste system. In case of Naranappa, he did everything which was against society, humanity and most importantly against religion. Naranappa strongly put his views to Praneshacharya:

> You read those lush sexy Puranas, but you preach a life of barrenness. But my words, they say what they mean: if I say sleep with a woman, it means sleep with a woman; if I say eat fish, it means eat fish. Can I give you Brahmins a piece of advice? Push those sickly wives of yours into the river. . . . And if you don't experience God when you wake up, my name isn't Naranappa. (25-26)

Under these undecided circumstances, the only motive behind the cremation is the gold offered by Chandri. Lakshmana and Garudacharya are the relatives of Naranappa who can perform the rites. Only for the sake of gold their wives scold them to perform the rites. So, both of them ask Praneshacharya to perform the rites. Now Praneshacharya once again is in dilemma, "if the problem of the dead man's rites should be solved, the problem of ornaments would not be solved." (34) Till now nobody is thinking about the dead body. Dasacharya, who lives next to Naranappa, requests Praneshacharya to take quick decision as the body is stinking. He suggests that without taking gold he can perform the rites along with four persons. Here once again the reason for Dasacharya's offer for the rites is his own hunger. He is a glutton and depends on the food given by the others.

Another interesting woman character portrayed in the novel is Lakshmidevamma. She is the oldest person in the village. She married at the age of eight, widowed at ten, her mother-in-law and father-in-law had died when she was fifteen, and before she was twenty her parents had also died. These tragic incidents made her life miserable and moreover people of Agrahara call her ill-omen. Garuda's father had taken custody of the little property and after his death Garuda is custodian of Lakshmi's property. Lakshmi's miserable condition makes her rebel against these societal norms. She shouts:

> You villain! A golden man like Naranappa became an outcaste—got himself a harlot. You fellows call yourself Brahmins, you sit there and don't want to take out a dead man's body. Where has your Brahminism gone, you rascals! In this Agrahara, in all my born days, have I seen a body kept uncremated all night? Not once. Brahminism is in ruins. (43)

Later on she shivered with terror and shouted, 'Naranappa's ghost! Naranappa's ghost!' She is terrified by the unseen imagined ghost of Naranappa.

Chandri waits for the verdict of Praneshacharya without proper food and sleep. Her ten years' companionship with Naranappa is not due to money and sexual pleasure, rather she is emotionally attached to him. Her only aim now is a proper funeral done by the Brahmin hands. She compares herself to Draupadi, who requested Lord Krishna (i.e. Praneshacharya) for help.

Not only is Chandri worried, Praneshacharya is also in search of proper solution to his dilemma. He is worried on many counts. First, he is afraid of admitting that the Book of Dharma has no solution to offer. Secondly, people will question him about his knowledge on the issue. As a Brahmin his primary aim is to protect his Dharma. He came outside and saw Chandri lying down in the verandah. He offered mat and pillow and returned all the gold which she had offered him for the cremation of Naranappa.

As the time passes, the dead body starts stinking; children and other people around Naranappa's house cannot bear the smell in the summer time. Women of Agrahara now start cursing Naranappa and they are also scared that Naranappa's ghost can harm their children. Everybody is tense and children count the numbers of rats near Naranappa's house. Naranappa's roaming ghost, bad smell of the dead body and young Brahmins' hunger compels them to think of the cremation. Meanwhile poor Chandri, afraid of facing the angry Brahmins of Agrahara, sits near the temple, waiting for the verdict of Praneshacharya.

Almost all the Brahmins of Agrahara are half-dead with hunger, waiting for Praneshacharya who is still inside the temple. Suddenly they see many vultures flying in the sky and picking the dead rats. Superstitious people believe that something drastic shall happen in such circumstances. Although coming of vultures for their food is a natural phenomenon but people of Agrahara are scared as if the soul of dead Naranappa is ready to take revenge. Even Sitadevi and Anasuya request their husbands:

> Let the gold go to hell! Why do we need other people's property? Please take out the body and get to the rites. Naranappa's spirit is calling out these vultures. (61)

Inside the temple Praneshacharya requests God to show a proper solution of this problem. Unable to find any positive answer, he returns to his house. It was dark in the forest and Praneshacharya heard the sound of bangles. Chandri wants to touch his feet but suddenly falls on him. Praneshacharya's first experience of woman's body makes him lose control on his body and soul.

In section two of the novel, Chandri is seen as a woman, lover and a kind human being. Her respect for Praneshacharya forces her to commit the sin in front of the Brahmins of Agrahara. Her first priority is to cremate the dead body. She is afraid of the orphaned and unprotected dead body of Naranappa but her humanity compels her to take a quick decision to cremate the body with the help of Muslim community. With the help of Ahmad Bari she keeps the dead body in the cart and moves to cremation ground and performs the rites and decides to leave the place forever.

Praneshacharya is not able to take any decision about the cremation and decides to accept his sin. Nobody knows about the dead body and Chandri. Praneshacharya suggests to other Brahmins to take the decision on their own. After this, he feels relieved and unburdened. The entire village decides to go to Kaimara for consultation on the issue. Next morning, while returning from Kaimara Dasacharya and Padmanabhacharya fall sick.

Praneshacharya's family stays alone in the Agrahara. Praneshacharya remembers his experience with Chandri. He searches for Chandri and comes back to his house. On returning home he finds his wife dead. He goes to Kaimara to gather people of Agrahara and cremate the dead body of his wife.

In the third and last section of the novel, Praneshacharya is disturbed by his own thoughts. His relation with Chandri, indecisiveness over the issue of Naranappa's cremation and his wife's death make him overburdened and restless. Suddenly he realizes that people of Agrahara must be waiting for him. Now he questions himself:

> Even if I leave everything behind, the community clings to me, asking me to fulfil the Brahmin is born to. It isn't easy to free oneself of this. . . . Shall I tell him I've sinned and lost the merits of penance? That I am no Brahmin? or just the simple truth? (96)

In order to overcome the burden of sin and guilt, he decides to go to Kundapura and stay with Chandri.

In the Agrahara, all the Brahmins decide to go the Naranappa's house for cremation. They arrange everything for the rites and wait for Praneshacharya. Till now no one knows that the dead body is not inside the house. When Praneshacharya hears the announcement by Municipality about the plague in Shivamogge, he once again thinks about his duties as a Brahmin and as a human being, "how shall I escape this state of neither here nor there, this ghostliness?" (131) Customs preserve our culture and transfer it to the succeeding generations, bring people together and develop social relationships among people. Praneshacharya's duty as a pure Brahmin of Agrahara is not only to show them the right way of religion and morality but also to protect the customs. Customs are essential to the life of a society and are held so sacred that any violation of them is regarded not only a crime upon the people, it also attracts the vengeance of God. The sense of guilt at having violated a moral principle is very close to the sense of sin even when the specific norm is not religiously sanctioned. Now he realizes that one must be aware not only of outward things but also of the inward movement of desires, motives, anxiety, fears and sorrows. Morality is concern of conscience and deals with the absolute standards of the whole of man's life. Praneshacharya's physical relationship with Chandri makes him realize that morality is concerned with good and evil. Considering his own action, Praneshacharya starts his journey to the Agrahara. For him, the case of Naranappa's cremation becomes unimportant and secondary. His struggle to save his religion and morality overshadows his inner guilt towards the society and his own wife. Although the novel ends without any resolution, the readers are forced to think about the social taboos, norms and evils which are standing like 'Himalaya' in front of an individual like Praneshacharya. A person of knowledge and wisdom, his own actions are now questionable, whereas Chandri, a lowcaste woman, fulfills her duties towards the person with whom she lived for more than ten years. As a faithful woman and good human being, she represents an ideal Indian woman.

NOTE

U.R. Anantha Murthy, *Samskara: A Rite for a Dead Man*, trans. A.K. Ramanujan (New Delhi: Oxford University Press).

Samskara as an Exploration of Man's Inner Experience

SURKHA DANGWAL
H.N.B. Garhwal University, Srinagar Garhwal

U.R. Anantha Murthy was born into a Brahmin family on 21 December 1932, in a village in Karnataka. He studied at Mysore and was awarded a Gold Medal for his master's degree. He was appointed a lecturer at the same University, and has continued to be a teacher of English literature for the greater part of his working life. He was supervised by Malcolm Bradbury at the University of Birmingham for his Ph.D. It was here he began to write and revise his first novel *Samskara* (1965), a story about a Brahmin priest faced with an existential choice after the death of a fellow Brahmin. The making of *Samskara* went through various stages.

At the time he was revising the first draft of *Samskara*, Bradbury took him to see Bergam's *The Seventh Seal*, which was being shown without subtitles; seeing the film as a series of dark images and in snatches of untranslated dialogue crystallized, for Anantha Murthy, the nature of the subject matter—a south Indian village; death and its aftermath; sex, metaphysics, and individual choice that he was working on, and pointed out a way as to how he should revise it.

The late D.R. Nagaraj, distinguished critic and commentator, divided Anantha Murthy's fiction into two phases. First is the 'radical' phase which belongs to the portrayal of rebels who transgress a boundary of caste, community and society. The second phase is actually the critique of what was dramatized in the earlier work and characterized by self-doubt. While this is pertinent, one also sees a continuity between an early work such as *Samskara*, and a relatively late one such as *Aidu Dashakara*

Kathegalu (Collected Stories). Both narratives are a record of the duress of the rational and high-minded values of the protagonist.

In *Samskara*, it is the dead Brahmin, Naranappa, who has led an irresponsible life, leading to an embarrassing and unpleasant situation after his death. None of the priests except the protagonist wishes to perform his death-rites. In the story, it is Anantha's friend, who by not having changed or evolved with modernity, presents an equally exasperating dilemma to the narrator. The text seems to allegorize Anantha Murthy's own dilemma and ambivalences as a writer. The dilemma is that he must write in a style that is rational, individualistic, even progressive, while the material from which he derives his vitality and inspiration can be seen to represent a retrograde form of existence, that is erotic, centred in community, and the vernacular. Anantha Murthy himself has said that his more rational and intellectual mental processes belong to the English language. This is the reason that he often writes his essays in English. But at the same time, his intention is to give entry to the unrecognized, local traditions through the back door.

The process of interrogating the Brahmin clan particularly and Hinduism in general, the novel opens to introduce the protagonist Praneshacharya; the most respected person of the agrahara (the exclusive orthodox colony of Brahmins). He went to Kashi, studied there and returned with the title "Crest-Jewel of Vedic Learning." He is the most learned priest and local guru of all the brahmins. They often use to turn to him for solutions of their problems. He is not only the preacher of *Bhagavadgita* but also believes in its practice. He had deliberately married an invalid and sick woman and is proud of his self-sacrifice:

> He bathed Bhagirathi's body, a dried-up wasted pea-pod, and wrapped a fresh sari around it; then he offered food and flowers to the gods as he did every day, put the flowers in her hair, and gave her holy water. She touched his feet, he blessed her. Then he brought her a bowlful of cracked wheat porridge from the kitchen. (1)

The narrative presents a contrast by introducing the other 'infamous' brahmin who lives in the same agrahara. His name is Naranappa. He had violated each and every norm of brahminhood. He broke every known taboo—drank liquor, ate fish, caught-fish with his Muslim friends in the holy temple tank and lived with a lowcaste woman Chandri. He has left his lawfully wedded wife. He is against every established institution like marriage and brahminhood. Whenever Praneshacharya gave him counsel he laughed and sneered at the brahmin ways: "Your texts and rites don't work any more. The Congress Party is coming to power, you'll have to open up the temples to all outcastes." (21) Naranappa did not find logic in living with a woman who was not able to give him pleasure even if she is a legitimate wife:

> O Acharya, who in the world can live with a girl who gives no pleasure—except of course some barren brahmins! . . . You fellows—you brahmins—you want to tie me down to a hysterical female, just because she is some relative, right? Just keep your dharma to yourself—we've but one life—I belong to the "Hedonist School" which says—Borrow, borrow and drink your ghee, as they say. (21)

By his deeds, his every effort is to destroy brahminism. Because of him one young man left Durvasapura and joined army. The brahmins of agrahara believe that in the army he is forced to eat beef. Only on the advice of Naranappa, another young man left his wife and home and joined a travelling group of singers and actors. His only sorrow that hardly anything of it is left to destroy, except for the brahminism of Praneshacharya. One day he advised Acharya:

> Acharya-re? Push those sickly wives of yours into the river. Be like the sages of your holy legends—get hold of a fish-scented Fisherwoman who can cook you fish-soup, and go to sleep in her arms. And if you don't experience God when you wake up, my name isn't Naranappa. (25)

To show the contrast between orthodox brahminism and anti-brahminism, due place is given to the dialogue between Naranappa and Praneshacharya. The ceaseless conflict between good and evil and the battle between Dharma and Adharma ended when Naranappa went to Shivamogge, a town far away from Durvasapura, and returned with high fever. Soon he developed a big lump and died within a couple of days.

The novel opens with the news of the death of Naranappa. Chandri comes to Praneshacharya to inform him of Naranappa's death. The novel deals with the problem which arises due to Naranappa's death. The problem is, "who should cremate Naranappa?" The cremation should take place immediately because only after the last rite, the villagers should eat food. Because Naranappa was Brahmin, he should be cremated only by a brahmin but to cremate such a brahmin as him, nobody wants to destroy his brahminhood. To solve their problem, all brahmins look up to Praneshacharya:

> We don't have to advise our great Praneshacharya. He knows all about alliances and misalliances, has studied it all in Kashi, he knows all the scriptures, earned the title Crest-Jewel of Vedic Learning. What do you say? . . . Our Acharya has won all sorts of arguments with all the super-pundits, yours and ours, won honours at every seat of learning in the South, fifteen lace shawls and silver platters . . . our Acharya. . . . what do you say? (5-6)

In order to find the answer of the overwhelming question related to Naranappa's death-rite, the Acharya goes under a metamorphosis of his inner 'self.' The dilemma of Acharya shows that Naranappa's character is a symbol of Acharya's self and not the opposite of it. In trying to resolve the problem, the Acharya reaches a turning point and feels a re-birth. The death of Naranappa is a re-birth of Praneshacharya. The novel primarily deals with the self-discovery of the protagonist. It is progressively more of inward voyage, where the novelist explores the inner life and 'self' of Praneshacharya. When Naranappa was alive, he raised certain questions against brahminhood and his mythological reminders are used by the novelist for greater richness and complexity of Acharya's self.

The narratology of the novel is conventional. The structure is built upon the scenes in the life of characters arranged systematically. The plot is tight and well-connected between the various incidents chosen as pegs to spread the structure on. So, we get a completely connected picture of Naranappa as well as Praneshacharya's life, which is the central organizing principle of the story. The narrative seems to cover many years, in fact the country's old traditions of brahmin community are projected through the orthodox Praneshacharya. If he talked to the lowcaste Chandri "he would have to bathe again before his meal." The actions described in the novel are to be measured both on internal and external value scales. The structure of the novel is shaped by the novelist's method of presenting the inner reality of the mind. The protagonist Praneshacharya's life is made of paradoxes.

Surprisingly, the conflict between the inner and outer selves of one's personality has always been prominent to Anantha Murthy. In an interview with Sachidananda Mohanty, he states:

> Most of us write because we enjoy solitude. I found that even children enjoy solitude. They want to play but at the same time they want to play with themselves. When I see my grandson talking to himself, I see the origin of my own writings. You want to talk to yourself. It is the moment when you discover that there is a Sakshi in you. In fact there are two selves: a self which participates in the play and a self that stands apart and watches, like the great image of the Upanishads, the bird which eats and the one that watches, the two golden birds. They are in all of us and are the source of all writings.

In fact, all the brahmin characters in the novels are jealous of Naranappa's forbidden pleasures. For the answer of the overwhelming question regarding the cremation of Naranappa, they all turn to Praneshacharya, the opposite of Naranappa. Ironically, in seeking the answer he goes through the forbidden pleasure and abandons everything and becomes one with his opposite. He sleeps with Chandri and finds himself misfit to preach the brahmins at agrahara anymore. It is this particular moment when he discovers that there is a Sakshi in him. At the moment he experiences all the stages right from his childhood to salvation. He wakes up feeling as if he has "fallen into his childhood, lying in his mother's lap." (67) He also feels "his boyhood desires." (83) The collective consciousness of his community suddenly shifts within his own body. The 'Samskara' of the brahminhood become his own 'Samskara' of transformation. His inner voyage proves that there is no division between 'collective' and 'individual' and 'outer' and 'inner.' The realization of the truth of his inner realities is shown through the change of place. The event of his worldly pleasures took place in the solitude. During the inner voyage:

> The Acharya did not return to the agrahara after his wife's cremation. He thought of nothing, neither the fifteen gold lace shawls in his box, the two hundred rupees, nor the basil-bread rosary done in gold given by the monastery. Meaning to walk wherever his legs took him, he walked towards the east.

Walking towards east is also symbolic of the 'orient,' where the possible solution could be found. The symbols and images are employed in the novel for confirming the realization and recovery of truth of one's self. The interrogation of the self highlights the real motive of the writer. When Praneshacharya interrogates himself:

> I must conduct my future differently, not deceive myself even one little bit. Why did I walk away after cremating my wife? The agrahara was stinking, one couldn't bear to return to it. Certainly a good reason: the intolerable stench in my nostril, the sense of pollution, certainly. Then what? Why didn't I want to meet again the brahmins who were waiting for my guidance? Why? (90)

The 'outer' pollution of agrahara represents the 'inner' pollution of Acharya himself. He wants to reveal the truth before the community but passing through different places his innermost self also recovers at the same time. His dilemma is to recover and realize the individual's 'self' and not only the role imposed by one's cast and community:

> I cannot escape fear. If I decided to live with Chandri without telling anyone, the decision is not complete, not fearless. I must come now to a final decision. All things indirect must become direct. Must pierce straight in the eye.

Again:

> But it's agony either way. If I hide things, all through life I'll be agonized by the fear of discovery, by some onlooking eye. If I don't, I'll muddy the lives of others by opening up and exposing the truth to the very eyes my brahminhood has lived and grown by.

At this point, the question of Naranappa's cremation has been taken over by the more important problem of Acharya's 'to be or not to be' state of mind. He is like Tiresias of *The Waste Land*, "throbbing between two lives." Like Tiresias, the Acharya brings together all the transformations and qualifies to summarize the experience he has gone through in the solitude. Like Tiresias, his one life, that is, 'Crest-Jewel of Vedic learning' is dead and the other powerless to be born. But at the same time Tiresias is gifted with a prophetic vision by seeing the nature of the 'dead' and the 'unborn.' Acharya's inner feelings of disgust and guilt, based on his own experience of forbidden pleasure, dominate his mind. His inward sufferings occupy his mind. It is not Naranappa but his self—the truth—that "stuck to him like a leech" (136) He wants to kill Naranappa inside his own consciousness:

> I'll stand exposed like the naked quick of life; and I, elder in their midst, will turn into a new man at midnight. Maybe when the fire leaps and dances around Naranappa's dead body, there'll be a certain consolation. When I tell them about myself, there should be no taint of repentance in me, no trace of any sorrow that I am a sinner. If not, I cannot go beyond conflict and dualities. (131-32)

Anantha Murthy believes that it is a must for a writer to "recover in solitude the truths of one's inner self." In searching the truth of his own inner experience, Praneshacharya decided to go back and "let things happen as they will." (123) At the end of the novel, there is the beginning of his journey back to home with an entirely different individual. Like a writer, the protagonist feels that ultimately it is not ideology but one's felt experience that should guide the individual. Here the ideology of an orthodox brahmin contrasts with a deeply felt experience of an individual who has gone through some strange passage of his life that he never felt and studied so far.

Finally the writer has tactfully used 'journey' as a metaphor to show the future course of action. It is only in a suggestive way with the help of "a silver of the moon" that "will appear over the hills" (134) after the new-moon day. His inner voyage finds expression through his outer travelling "for another four or five hours." (138) The concluding line shows the continuity of his inner voyage but at the same time the word "expectant" is used perhaps for the recovery of Praneshacharya's dilemma and guilt and make the reader more expectant than ever before. The novel ends with a question, "Then after that what?" as it opens with a question that remained unanswered. In such instances the science of psychology, the power of poetry and the art of rhetoric are combined to make the structure of the language of narrative peculiarly suited to a novel like *Samskara*. Perhaps the first and last questions of the novel are answered in the following lines of T.S. Eliot:

> The world turns and the world changes.
> But one thing does not change.
> In all of my years, one thing does not change.
> However you disguise it, this thing does not change.
> The perpetual struggle of God and Evil. ("The Rock," 1934)

Works Cited

Anantha Murthy, U.R. 1978. *Samskara*. New Delhi: Oxford University Press.

Chaudhuri, Amit. 2001. *The Picador Book of Modern Indian Literature*. London: Picador.

Eliot, T.S. 1968. *The Complete Poems and Plays of T.S. Eliot*. London: Faber and Faber.

Summerhill IIAS Review. 2002. Vol. VIII, No. 1, Summer. Shimla: Indian Institute of Advanced Study.

Samskara: Some Critical Observations

RAMA KUNDU
Burdwan University, Burdwan

Graham Swift's *Last Orders* (1996) is the story of the last rites of a person. The four friends of Jack Dodds, an ex-soldier in the Second World War and former London butcher, set out on their bizarre trip in order to carry out the last wishes of the dear deceased regarding the disposal of his last physical remains. Jack Dodds' four friends arrive at Margate's pier at their journey's end, holding the jar containing Jack's ashes, because this was Jack's expressed wish. It is a long pier, but Jack had specified the end. So they proceed. This last chapter is in Ray's voice, Ray who had been the best friend and also something more, something else. The rough weather, the incoming waves, the high wind cannot deter them; at the same time they are also lashed by waves of memories.

> We can't speak, strung out from each other, but I reckon I couldn't speak anyway. Because there's something swelling up inside me, in my chest, where I'm holding Jack under my car-coat, like there's waves beating at my own harbour wall. (289)

But at this moment he is not his own master, as it were. Something else has taken control over him, "telling me what to do, telling me how to act." (290) They make for the specified point under the relentless rain; as they finally reach, there's a moment's respite—almost like a 'sign.' This is also a kind of ritual, keeping your hands dry, "it's so Jack don't stick to us, it's so we don't get Jack stuck to our hands," (293) while throwing the ash "like scattering seed," (293) "like white soft sand on a beach." (294) They all throw their handfuls at the same time without looking at each other, saying 'Goodbye Jack,' "say[ing] it to the wind," (294) and "the wind takes it, it's gone in a whirl, in a flash." (294) Ray scoops up the last two handfuls, saying 'Goodbye Jack.' Then

> The sky and the sea and the wind are all mixed up together but I reckon it wouldn't make no difference if they weren't because of the blur in my eyes . . . and, the ash that I carried in my hands, which was the Jack who once walked around, is carried away by the wind, is whirled away by the wind till the ash becomes wind and the wind becomes Jack what we're made of. (294-95)

What an appropriate ending for the story of a 'last order'! Indeed it is difficult to imagine or wish for a better death rite, more emotionally-aesthetically satisfying or more beautiful!

Last Orders has been compared with Faulkner's *As I Lay Dying*—even insinuatingly[1] sometimes—to the understandable annoyance of the author. Like Jack's friends in Swift's novel, the husband and children of Addie in Faulkner's story undertake a long and hazardous journey in order to give the dead [already rotting] body a burial according to the deceased's 'last order.' From contrary perspectives the two sets of mourners [Swift's and Faulkner's] eventually arrive at a vision that encompasses and surpasses both life and death.

Burial/cremation rites have indeed been an age-old preoccupation in literature which continues to surface through ages—be it sophisticated and modern literature or simple and communal folk art. One can look as far back as the *Iliad*, and recall the old king Prium, appealing as a bereaved father to Achilles for the dead body of his son Hector, so that he can perform the appropriate last rites. The basic issue of Sophocles's *Antigone* is the dead man's claim or lack of claim to proper death rites. The elaborate rituals regarding the 'Burial of the Dead'[2] forms one of the major themes of traditional English and Scottish ballads, while Achebe's *Things Fall Apart* invites us to consider the same subject from another angle—when an unusual death deprives the dead of the normal obsequies.

Anantha Murthy's *Samskara*—the very title denoting a Sanskrit term that literally means death-rites—thus can be placed in this long literary tradition. In a sense it is another story on the same age-old theme: the issue of the disposal of a dead body in an appropriate/adequate manner and the difficulties faced by the survivors under the specific circumstances. The circumstances in the present case are trying since they involve the death of a man who had been a non-conformist, a 'sinner,' a publicly condemned yet daring person who did not care for the condemnation or approbation of the community. Naranappa had, of course, left no such articulated instruction as the protagonists of Graham Swift or William Faulkner had done. Before Naranappa passed away under a sudden attack of plague he had lived a full life with all the attainable sensual pleasures that could be attained by an uninhibited hedonist in an obsoure corner of the country. Naranappa in his life and ways manifested the 'Rebel' spirit [*a la* Camus]; he had challenged the Brahmins in the 'agrahara' to excommunicate him; and they had not dared. Naranappa had defied all the rules laid down by the orthodox customs and scriptures regarding food, drink, sex and religiosity; he had openly taken a mistress from the 'untouchable' community. Therefore, after his sudden death none in the 'agrahara' can initially summon the courage or inclination to perform his cremation rites. The author, from his omniscient point of view, brings out the motives of Naranappa's clan-members, the fellow-Brahmins in the *agrahara*—motives governing their initial unwillingness and subsequent vacillation—with unconcealed irony. It is also part of the irony that after being left there for days at a stretch, spreading foul stench and infection, while the orthodox Brahmins go on discussing and debating the subtle points of the issue of cremation, the corpse is eventually disposed of—secretly and unceremoniously—under the cover of night and is burnt down through the joint venture of a pair of outcasts—a so-called untouchable woman and a Muslim friend of Naranappa. Ahmad Bari, the fish-merchant, remembers Naranappa, who is condemned by his own clan, with gratitude for helping him in a time of need. So he

> came at once with his bullock-cart, secretly loaded both the body and the firewood into it, drove to the cremation-ground before anyone knew, kindled a flapping flaming fire in the dark night and

> burned it to ashes—and left, twisting his bullocks' tails, goading them with various noises to run faster. (70)

The very bareness of the description proves eloquent; the absent [in a Derridean manner] becomes vividly present by not being present at all. There is no one to chant the *mantra*, burn incense, or pour holy water by the pyre. Naranappa, who had lived like a king, having his way in everything he wanted, passed away alone; his journey back to the elements is the most forlorn, alienated Passover.

Considered at another level, however, *Samskara* is much more than the story of one Naranappa's *Samskara* or death rites; it is indeed, as much, if not more, the story of Praneshacharya, who seems to have represented the counterpoint to Naranappa in every respect till the crisis that came in the wake of Naranappa's death. This crisis forces him to face himself. After years of abstinence—self-glorifying, proud and lonely[3]—he comes to recognize another hidden self, raising its hood within him, and this brings him face to face with an existential crisis. After the night with Chandri in the forest adjacent to the temple, Praneshacharya realizes:

> We shape ourselves through our choices, bring form and line to this thing we call our person. Naranappa became the person he chose to be. I chose to be something else and lived by it. But suddenly I turned at some turning. I'm not free till I realize that the turning is also my act, I'm to answer for it. What happened at that turning? Dualities, conflict, rushed into my own life. I hung suspended between two truths, like Trishanku. (98)

Is this not the same perception which Albert Camus registered when he wrote in his 1955 preface to *L'Etranger* that the book was concerned with "the truth of what we are and what we feel . . . without which no conquest of ourselves or of the world will ever be possible." (cited Thody 44)

Anantha Murthy's protagonist Praneshacharya is made to confront truth through a catastrophic event—an outbreak of plague. An important recurring theme of European and indigenous literature has been significantly exploited by the author of

Samskara; it is a dreaded sickness, i.e., the plague, which is made to assume metaphorical and supra-metaphorical significances in the context of the story, and can be usefully compared to Albert Camus's *La Peste*. It is not only that Praneshacharya, like Camus' Father Paneloux, is the only character in the novel who confronts a genuine intellectual-moral crisis brought about by the catastrophe, and thereby travels a long way from complacent religious orthodoxy to an existential angst, from happy certainty to an agonized quest for selfhood; the plague, as a real event as well as a powerful image, has also been elaborately inscribed into the texture of the First Part of the novel. Even scenically the location is—like that of Camus's novel—shabby, seedy, dusty, foul-smelling, rotting, and continuously dotted and re-dotted by scouring and dying rats, which do not allow the reader a chance to forget about the disease they carry. The sky, hanging over the scene, is dotted with vultures, "omen of death" (59), which add the element of horror to the pervasive dread. Chapter IX presents a fascinating close-up of this scene of horror, complete with vultures pouncing upon dead/dying rats. For instance,

> Garudacharya lifted his head and looked into the dazzling heat above. He saw vultures, vultures, vultures in the blue blue sky reeling, gliding, spiralling circle below circle, descending. (59)
> Another vulture, flying far in the sky, came down to sit on Naranappa's house. He lifted his head, flapped his demon wings loudly, came to a standstill and inspected the whole agrahara with his eagle eyes. After that, more flying vultures came down to sit, two by two, two on each house, as if they had agreed on it earlier. Some would whirr to the ground unpredictably, pick up rats in their beak and perch back on the roof to peck at their prey at leisure. (60)
> The air was still, not a leaf was stirring. The only moving things were the gently gliding vultures in the clear blue sky. (61)

This elaborate evocation of sickness, death and rot, through the concrete animal imagery, further reinforces the suggestion that the plague is a physical disease as well as a symptom of the rot of a decadent society and world, which will eventually destroy the Brahmin and the 'untouchable,' man and woman, even human and non-human, without discrimination. All the bronze gongs and conches, supposed to be used for household worship, and now used to chase vultures, suggest—with a tinge of grim comicality—the pitiful ineffectuality of feeble, half-hearted measures to root out the stem.

Finally, precisely because it is plague which is the bringer of death here, tragedy ceases to be an isolated individual event; it assumes a collective nature; plague, thus, becomes symptomatic of a societal, pervasive, collective sickness from which only a collective sharing at cleansing, a collective '*Samskara*' can provide a way out. As Camus wrote in his essay "*L'Homme révolté*":

> In the experience of the absurd, tragedy is an individual event. From the moment that the movement of revolt takes place, this tragedy becomes aware of its collective nature. It is an adventure in which everybody is involved. The first step forward for a mind possessed with the idea of the strangeness of the world . . . lies in the recognition that it shares this strangeness with all other men and that human reality, as a whole, suffers from this distance from itself and from the world. The evil which, up to then, had been experienced by one man becomes a plague affecting everyone [une peste collective] (cited Thody 44)

Samskara, however, unlike *La Peste*, is not a mythic novel, not even an allegoric one. It is rooted in the reality of countryside India which is not yet obliterated altogether. At the same time the novel embraces certain perennial themes and issues. *La Peste* has been described by Camus' critic as 'an attempt to understand his time' (Thody 74). *Samskara*, written during a turning point of India's political-social-cultural transition, can be described as its author's attempt to understand his own time, and also to see his own time in relation to all times and life in general, even if the perception brings no assurance or promise.

It is useful to note that the novel ends on a note of bafflement rather than certainty, questions surge up but only to be left unresolved; wisdom remains denied. Under the star-studded sky of early dawn, with its silver moon and the constellation of the

Seven Sages, a sign of supreme wisdom, the uncertain sojourner travels on:

> He will travel, for another four or five hours. Then, after that, what? Praneshacharya waited, anxious, expectant. (138)

It is perhaps only in the fitness of things that the novel should "end", but "not conclude." (147)

NOTES

1. Salman Rushdie refers to the 'media roasting' of Graham Swift for 'plundering' Faulkner's *As I Lay Dying* in his *Last Orders*. Interestingly Faulkner himself had been accused of 'borrowing' its structure from Hawthorne's *The Scarlet Letter*. Rushdie writes, "His [Faulkner's] retort is the best possible answer that could be given: that when he was in the throes of composing what he modestly called his 'tour-de-force,' he took whatever he needed from wherever he could find it, and knew of no writer who would not find such borrowing to be completely justified." (*Step* 72-73).
2. Eliot scoops up the phrase from the Book of Common Prayer, which was used on the occasion of the burial ceremony at the Church of London.
3. The author gives unambiguous hints about the irony implicit in Praneshacharya's practice of abstinence and Brahminic 'duties'; for instance,

> The Acharya nursed his invalid wife to uphold the great mercy of god, bore up with Naranappa's misdeeds, dispersed little by little the darkness in the brahmins' heads filled with chants they did not understand. His duties in this world grew lighter and more fragrant like sandalwood rubbed daily on stone. (17)

Works Cited

Anantha Murthy, U.R. *Samskara*. Delhi: Oxford India Paperbacks, 1978.

Rushdie, S. "Influence" *Step across this Line*. London: Vintage, 2003.

Swift, Graham. *Last Orders*. London: Picador, 1996.

Thody, Philip. *Albert Camus*. London: Macmillan, 1989.